GNU Make

GNU Make

A Program for Directing Recompilation
GNU make Version 3.77
July 1998

Richard M. Stallman and Roland McGrath

Short Contents

1	Overview of **make**	1
2	An Introduction to Makefiles	3
3	Writing Makefiles	11
4	Writing Rules	17
5	Writing the Commands in Rules	37
6	How to Use Variables	51
7	Conditional Parts of Makefiles	65
8	Functions for Transforming Text	71
9	How to Run **make**	83
10	Using Implicit Rules	95
11	Using **make** to Update Archive Files	115
12	Features of GNU **make**	119
13	Incompatibilities and Missing Features	123
14	Makefile Conventions	125
Appendix A	Quick Reference	139
Appendix B	Errors Generated by Make	145
Appendix C	Complex Makefile Example	149
Index of Concepts		155
Index of Functions, Variables, & Directives		165

Table of Contents

1 Overview of make **1**
  1.1 How to Read This Manual 1
  1.2 Problems and Bugs 2

2 An Introduction to Makefiles **3**
  2.1 What a Rule Looks Like 3
  2.2 A Simple Makefile 4
  2.3 How make Processes a Makefile 5
  2.4 Variables Make Makefiles Simpler 6
  2.5 Letting make Deduce the Commands 7
  2.6 Another Style of Makefile 8
  2.7 Rules for Cleaning the Directory 9

3 Writing Makefiles **11**
  3.1 What Makefiles Contain 11
  3.2 What Name to Give Your Makefile 11
  3.3 Including Other Makefiles 12
  3.4 The Variable MAKEFILES 13
  3.5 How Makefiles Are Remade 14
  3.6 Overriding Part of Another Makefile 15

4 Writing Rules **17**
  4.1 Rule Syntax 17
  4.2 Using Wildcard Characters in File Names 18
      4.2.1 Wildcard Examples 18
      4.2.2 Pitfalls of Using Wildcards 19
      4.2.3 The Function wildcard 20
  4.3 Searching Directories for Dependencies 21
      4.3.1 VPATH: Search Path for All Dependencies 21
      4.3.2 The vpath Directive 21
      4.3.3 How Directory Searches are Performed 23
      4.3.4 Writing Shell Commands with Directory Search .. 24
      4.3.5 Directory Search and Implicit Rules 24
      4.3.6 Directory Search for Link Libraries 25
  4.4 Phony Targets 25
  4.5 Rules without Commands or Dependencies 27
  4.6 Empty Target Files to Record Events 27
  4.7 Special Built-in Target Names 28
  4.8 Multiple Targets in a Rule 30

4.9   Multiple Rules for One Target 30
4.10   Static Pattern Rules 31
       4.10.1   Syntax of Static Pattern Rules 31
       4.10.2   Static Pattern Rules versus Implicit Rules 33
4.11   Double-Colon Rules 34
4.12   Generating Dependencies Automatically 34

5   Writing the Commands in Rules 37

5.1   Command Echoing 37
5.2   Command Execution 38
5.3   Parallel Execution 39
5.4   Errors in Commands 40
5.5   Interrupting or Killing make 42
5.6   Recursive Use of make 42
       5.6.1   How the MAKE Variable Works 43
       5.6.2   Communicating Variables to a Sub-make 44
       5.6.3   Communicating Options to a Sub-make 46
       5.6.4   The '--print-directory' Option 47
5.7   Defining Canned Command Sequences 48
5.8   Using Empty Commands 49

6   How to Use Variables 51

6.1   Basics of Variable References 51
6.2   The Two Flavors of Variables 52
6.3   Advanced Features for Reference to Variables 55
       6.3.1   Substitution References 55
       6.3.2   Computed Variable Names 55
6.4   How Variables Get Their Values 58
6.5   Setting Variables 58
6.6   Appending More Text to Variables 59
6.7   The override Directive 61
6.8   Defining Variables Verbatim 61
6.9   Variables from the Environment 62
6.10   Target-specific Variable Values 63
6.11   Pattern-specific Variable Values 64

7   Conditional Parts of Makefiles 65

7.1   Example of a Conditional 65
7.2   Syntax of Conditionals 66
7.3   Conditionals that Test Flags 68

8   Functions for Transforming Text 71

8.1   Function Call Syntax 71
8.2   Functions for String Substitution and Analysis 72
8.3   Functions for File Names 75
8.4   The `foreach` Function 78
8.5   The `origin` Function 79
8.6   The `shell` Function 81

9   How to Run make 83

9.1   Arguments to Specify the Makefile 83
9.2   Arguments to Specify the Goals 83
9.3   Instead of Executing the Commands 85
9.4   Avoiding Recompilation of Some Files 87
9.5   Overriding Variables 87
9.6   Testing the Compilation of a Program 88
9.7   Summary of Options 89

10   Using Implicit Rules 95

10.1   Using Implicit Rules 95
10.2   Catalogue of Implicit Rules 96
10.3   Variables Used by Implicit Rules 100
10.4   Chains of Implicit Rules 102
10.5   Defining and Redefining Pattern Rules 103
        10.5.1   Introduction to Pattern Rules 104
        10.5.2   Pattern Rule Examples 105
        10.5.3   Automatic Variables 106
        10.5.4   How Patterns Match 108
        10.5.5   Match-Anything Pattern Rules 109
        10.5.6   Canceling Implicit Rules 110
10.6   Defining Last-Resort Default Rules 110
10.7   Old-Fashioned Suffix Rules 111
10.8   Implicit Rule Search Algorithm 112

11   Using make to Update Archive Files 115

11.1   Archive Members as Targets 115
11.2   Implicit Rule for Archive Member Targets 115
        11.2.1   Updating Archive Symbol Directories 116
11.3   Dangers When Using Archives 117
11.4   Suffix Rules for Archive Files 117

12   Features of GNU make 119

13   Incompatibilities and Missing Features ... 123

14   Makefile Conventions 125
    14.1   General Conventions for Makefiles 125
    14.2   Utilities in Makefiles 126
    14.3   Variables for Specifying Commands 127
    14.4   Variables for Installation Directories 128
    14.5   Standard Targets for Users 132
    14.6   Install Command Categories 137

Appendix A   Quick Reference 139

Appendix B   Errors Generated by Make 145

Appendix C   Complex Makefile Example 149

Index of Concepts 155

Index of Functions, Variables, & Directives ... 165

1 Overview of make

The make utility automatically determines which pieces of a large program need to be recompiled, and issues commands to recompile them. This manual describes GNU make, which was implemented by Richard Stallman and Roland McGrath. GNU make conforms to section 6.2 of *IEEE Standard 1003.2-1992* (POSIX.2).

Our examples show C programs, since they are most common, but you can use make with any programming language whose compiler can be run with a shell command. Indeed, make is not limited to programs. You can use it to describe any task where some files must be updated automatically from others whenever the others change.

To prepare to use make, you must write a file called the *makefile* that describes the relationships among files in your program and provides commands for updating each file. In a program, typically, the executable file is updated from object files, which are in turn made by compiling source files.

Once a suitable makefile exists, each time you change some source files, this simple shell command:

```
make
```

suffices to perform all necessary recompilations. The make program uses the makefile data base and the last-modification times of the files to decide which of the files need to be updated. For each of those files, it issues the commands recorded in the data base.

You can provide command line arguments to make to control which files should be recompiled, or how. See Chapter 9 [How to Run make], page 83.

1.1 How to Read This Manual

If you are new to make, or are looking for a general introduction, read the first few sections of each chapter, skipping the later sections. In each chapter, the first few sections contain introductory or general information and the later sections contain specialized or technical information. The exception is Chapter 2 [An Introduction to Makefiles], page 3, all of which is introductory.

If you are familiar with other make programs, see Chapter 12 [Features of GNU make], page 119, which lists the enhancements GNU make has, and Chapter 13 [Incompatibilities and Missing Features], page 123, which explains the few things GNU make lacks that others have.

For a quick summary, see Section 9.7 [Options Summary], page 89, Appendix A [Quick Reference], page 139, and Section 4.7 [Special Targets], page 28.

1.2 Problems and Bugs

If you have problems with GNU make or think you've found a bug, please report it to the developers; we cannot promise to do anything but we might well want to fix it.

Before reporting a bug, make sure you've actually found a real bug. Carefully reread the documentation and see if it really says you can do what you're trying to do. If it's not clear whether you should be able to do something or not, report that too; it's a bug in the documentation!

Before reporting a bug or trying to fix it yourself, try to isolate it to the smallest possible makefile that reproduces the problem. Then send us the makefile and the exact results make gave you. Also say what you expected to occur; this will help us decide whether the problem was really in the documentation.

Once you've got a precise problem, please send electronic mail to:

        bug-make@gnu.org

Please include the version number of make you are using. You can get this information with the command 'make --version'. Be sure also to include the type of machine and operating system you are using. If possible, include the contents of the file 'config.h' that is generated by the configuration process.

2 An Introduction to Makefiles

You need a file called a *makefile* to tell **make** what to do. Most often, the makefile tells **make** how to compile and link a program.

In this chapter, we will discuss a simple makefile that describes how to compile and link a text editor which consists of eight C source files and three header files. The makefile can also tell **make** how to run miscellaneous commands when explicitly asked (for example, to remove certain files as a clean-up operation). To see a more complex example of a makefile, see Appendix C [Complex Makefile], page 149.

When **make** recompiles the editor, each changed C source file must be recompiled. If a header file has changed, each C source file that includes the header file must be recompiled to be safe. Each compilation produces an object file corresponding to the source file. Finally, if any source file has been recompiled, all the object files, whether newly made or saved from previous compilations, must be linked together to produce the new executable editor.

2.1 What a Rule Looks Like

A simple makefile consists of "rules" with the following shape:

```
target ... : dependencies ...
        command
        ...
        ...
```

A *target* is usually the name of a file that is generated by a program; examples of targets are executable or object files. A target can also be the name of an action to carry out, such as 'clean' (see Section 4.4 [Phony Targets], page 25).

A *dependency* is a file that is used as input to create the target. A target often depends on several files.

A *command* is an action that **make** carries out. A rule may have more than one command, each on its own line. **Please note:** you need to put a tab character at the beginning of every command line! This is an obscurity that catches the unwary.

Usually a command is in a rule with dependencies and serves to create a target file if any of the dependencies change. However, the rule that specifies commands for the target need not have dependencies. For example, the rule containing the delete command associated with the target 'clean' does not have dependencies.

A *rule*, then, explains how and when to remake certain files which are the targets of the particular rule. **make** carries out the commands on the dependencies to create or update the target. A rule can also explain how and when to carry out an action. See Chapter 4 [Writing Rules], page 17.

A makefile may contain other text besides rules, but a simple makefile need only contain rules. Rules may look somewhat more complicated than shown in this template, but all fit the pattern more or less.

2.2 A Simple Makefile

Here is a straightforward makefile that describes the way an executable file called `edit` depends on eight object files which, in turn, depend on eight C source and three header files.

In this example, all the C files include 'defs.h', but only those defining editing commands include 'command.h', and only low level files that change the editor buffer include 'buffer.h'.

```
edit : main.o kbd.o command.o display.o \
       insert.o search.o files.o utils.o
        cc -o edit main.o kbd.o command.o display.o \
                  insert.o search.o files.o utils.o

main.o : main.c defs.h
        cc -c main.c
kbd.o : kbd.c defs.h command.h
        cc -c kbd.c
command.o : command.c defs.h command.h
        cc -c command.c
display.o : display.c defs.h buffer.h
        cc -c display.c
insert.o : insert.c defs.h buffer.h
        cc -c insert.c
search.o : search.c defs.h buffer.h
        cc -c search.c
files.o : files.c defs.h buffer.h command.h
        cc -c files.c
utils.o : utils.c defs.h
        cc -c utils.c
clean :
        rm edit main.o kbd.o command.o display.o \
           insert.o search.o files.o utils.o
```

We split each long line into two lines using backslash-newline; this is like using one long line, but is easier to read.

To use this makefile to create the executable file called 'edit', type:

```
make
```

To use this makefile to delete the executable file and all the object files from the directory, type:

```
make clean
```

In the example makefile, the targets include the executable file 'edit', and the object files 'main.o' and 'kbd.o'. The dependencies are files such as 'main.c' and 'defs.h'. In fact, each '.o' file is both a target and a dependency. Commands include 'cc -c main.c' and 'cc -c kbd.c'.

When a target is a file, it needs to be recompiled or relinked if any of its dependencies change. In addition, any dependencies that are themselves automatically generated should be updated first. In this example, 'edit' depends on each of the eight object files; the object file 'main.o' depends on the source file 'main.c' and on the header file 'defs.h'.

A shell command follows each line that contains a target and dependencies. These shell commands say how to update the target file. A tab character must come at the beginning of every command line to distinguish commands lines from other lines in the makefile. (Bear in mind that make does not know anything about how the commands work. It is up to you to supply commands that will update the target file properly. All make does is execute the commands in the rule you have specified when the target file needs to be updated.)

The target 'clean' is not a file, but merely the name of an action. Since you normally do not want to carry out the actions in this rule, 'clean' is not a dependency of any other rule. Consequently, make never does anything with it unless you tell it specifically. Note that this rule not only is not a dependency, it also does not have any dependencies, so the only purpose of the rule is to run the specified commands. Targets that do not refer to files but are just actions are called *phony targets*. See Section 4.4 [Phony Targets], page 25, for information about this kind of target. See Section 5.4 [Errors in Commands], page 40, to see how to cause make to ignore errors from rm or any other command.

2.3 How make Processes a Makefile

By default, make starts with the first target (not targets whose names start with '.'). This is called the *default goal*. (*Goals* are the targets that make strives ultimately to update. See Section 9.2 [Arguments to Specify the Goals], page 83.)

In the simple example of the previous section, the default goal is to update the executable program 'edit'; therefore, we put that rule first.

Thus, when you give the command:

```
make
```

make reads the makefile in the current directory and begins by processing the first rule. In the example, this rule is for relinking 'edit'; but before

make can fully process this rule, it must process the rules for the files that 'edit' depends on, which in this case are the object files. Each of these files is processed according to its own rule. These rules say to update each '.o' file by compiling its source file. The recompilation must be done if the source file, or any of the header files named as dependencies, is more recent than the object file, or if the object file does not exist.

The other rules are processed because their targets appear as dependencies of the goal. If some other rule is not depended on by the goal (or anything it depends on, etc.), that rule is not processed, unless you tell **make** to do so (with a command such as **make clean**).

Before recompiling an object file, **make** considers updating its dependencies, the source file and header files. This makefile does not specify anything to be done for them—the '.c' and '.h' files are not the targets of any rules—so **make** does nothing for these files. But **make** would update automatically generated C programs, such as those made by Bison or Yacc, by their own rules at this time.

After recompiling whichever object files need it, **make** decides whether to relink 'edit'. This must be done if the file 'edit' does not exist, or if any of the object files are newer than it. If an object file was just recompiled, it is now newer than 'edit', so 'edit' is relinked.

Thus, if we change the file 'insert.c' and run **make**, **make** will compile that file to update 'insert.o', and then link 'edit'. If we change the file 'command.h' and run **make**, **make** will recompile the object files 'kbd.o', 'command.o' and 'files.o' and then link the file 'edit'.

2.4 Variables Make Makefiles Simpler

In our example, we had to list all the object files twice in the rule for 'edit' (repeated here):

```
edit : main.o kbd.o command.o display.o \
            insert.o search.o files.o utils.o
        cc -o edit main.o kbd.o command.o display.o \
            insert.o search.o files.o utils.o
```

Such duplication is error-prone; if a new object file is added to the system, we might add it to one list and forget the other. We can eliminate the risk and simplify the makefile by using a variable. *Variables* allow a text string to be defined once and substituted in multiple places later (see Chapter 6 [How to Use Variables], page 51).

It is standard practice for every makefile to have a variable named objects, OBJECTS, objs, OBJS, obj, or OBJ which is a list of all object file names. We would define such a variable objects with a line like this in the makefile:

```
objects = main.o kbd.o command.o display.o \
          insert.o search.o files.o utils.o
```

Then, each place we want to put a list of the object file names, we can substitute the variable's value by writing '$(objects)' (see Chapter 6 [How to Use Variables], page 51).

Here is how the complete simple makefile looks when you use a variable for the object files:

```
objects = main.o kbd.o command.o display.o \
          insert.o search.o files.o utils.o

edit : $(objects)
        cc -o edit $(objects)
main.o : main.c defs.h
        cc -c main.c
kbd.o : kbd.c defs.h command.h
        cc -c kbd.c
command.o : command.c defs.h command.h
        cc -c command.c
display.o : display.c defs.h buffer.h
        cc -c display.c
insert.o : insert.c defs.h buffer.h
        cc -c insert.c
search.o : search.c defs.h buffer.h
        cc -c search.c
files.o : files.c defs.h buffer.h command.h
        cc -c files.c
utils.o : utils.c defs.h
        cc -c utils.c
clean :
        rm edit $(objects)
```

2.5 Letting make Deduce the Commands

It is not necessary to spell out the commands for compiling the individual C source files, because make can figure them out: it has an *implicit rule* for updating a '.o' file from a correspondingly named '.c' file using a 'cc -c' command. For example, it will use the command 'cc -c main.c -o main.o' to compile 'main.c' into 'main.o'. We can therefore omit the commands from the rules for the object files. See Chapter 10 [Using Implicit Rules], page 95.

When a '.c' file is used automatically in this way, it is also automatically added to the list of dependencies. We can therefore omit the '.c' files from the dependencies, provided we omit the commands.

Here is the entire example, with both of these changes, and a variable `objects` as suggested above:

```
objects = main.o kbd.o command.o display.o \
          insert.o search.o files.o utils.o

edit : $(objects)
        cc -o edit $(objects)

main.o : defs.h
kbd.o : defs.h command.h
command.o : defs.h command.h
display.o : defs.h buffer.h
insert.o : defs.h buffer.h
search.o : defs.h buffer.h
files.o : defs.h buffer.h command.h
utils.o : defs.h

.PHONY : clean
clean :
        -rm edit $(objects)
```

This is how we would write the makefile in actual practice. (The complications associated with 'clean' are described elsewhere. See Section 4.4 [Phony Targets], page 25, and Section 5.4 [Errors in Commands], page 40.)

Because implicit rules are so convenient, they are important. You will see them used frequently.

2.6 Another Style of Makefile

When the objects of a makefile are created only by implicit rules, an alternative style of makefile is possible. In this style of makefile, you group entries by their dependencies instead of by their targets. Here is what one looks like:

```
objects = main.o kbd.o command.o display.o \
          insert.o search.o files.o utils.o

edit : $(objects)
        cc -o edit $(objects)

$(objects) : defs.h
kbd.o command.o files.o : command.h
display.o insert.o search.o files.o : buffer.h
```

Here 'defs.h' is given as a dependency of all the object files; 'command.h' and 'buffer.h' are dependencies of the specific object files listed for them.

Whether this is better is a matter of taste: it is more compact, but some people dislike it because they find it clearer to put all the information about each target in one place.

2.7 Rules for Cleaning the Directory

Compiling a program is not the only thing you might want to write rules for. Makefiles commonly tell how to do a few other things besides compiling a program: for example, how to delete all the object files and executables so that the directory is 'clean'.

Here is how we could write a make rule for cleaning our example editor:

```
clean:
        rm edit $(objects)
```

In practice, we might want to write the rule in a somewhat more complicated manner to handle unanticipated situations. We would do this:

```
.PHONY : clean
clean :
        -rm edit $(objects)
```

This prevents make from getting confused by an actual file called 'clean' and causes it to continue in spite of errors from rm. (See Section 4.4 [Phony Targets], page 25, and Section 5.4 [Errors in Commands], page 40.)

A rule such as this should not be placed at the beginning of the makefile, because we do not want it to run by default! Thus, in the example makefile, we want the rule for edit, which recompiles the editor, to remain the default goal.

Since clean is not a dependency of edit, this rule will not run at all if we give the command 'make' with no arguments. In order to make the rule run, we have to type 'make clean'. See Chapter 9 [How to Run make], page 83.

3 Writing Makefiles

The information that tells **make** how to recompile a system comes from reading a data base called the *makefile*.

3.1 What Makefiles Contain

Makefiles contain five kinds of things: *explicit rules*, *implicit rules*, *variable definitions*, *directives*, and *comments*. Rules, variables, and directives are described at length in later chapters.

- An *explicit rule* says when and how to remake one or more files, called the rule's targets. It lists the other files that the targets *depend on*, and may also give commands to use to create or update the targets. See Chapter 4 [Writing Rules], page 17.

- An *implicit rule* says when and how to remake a class of files based on their names. It describes how a target may depend on a file with a name similar to the target and gives commands to create or update such a target. See Chapter 10 [Using Implicit Rules], page 95.

- A *variable definition* is a line that specifies a text string value for a variable that can be substituted into the text later. The simple makefile example shows a variable definition for **objects** as a list of all object files (see Section 2.4 [Variables Make Makefiles Simpler], page 6).

- A *directive* is a command for **make** to do something special while reading the makefile. These include:

  - Reading another makefile (see Section 3.3 [Including Other Makefiles], page 12).

  - Deciding (based on the values of variables) whether to use or ignore a part of the makefile (see Chapter 7 [Conditional Parts of Makefiles], page 65).

  - Defining a variable from a verbatim string containing multiple lines (see Section 6.8 [Defining Variables Verbatim], page 61).

- '#' in a line of a makefile starts a *comment*. It and the rest of the line are ignored, except that a trailing backslash not escaped by another backslash will continue the comment across multiple lines. Comments may appear on any of the lines in the makefile, except within a **define** directive, and perhaps within commands (where the shell decides what is a comment). A line containing just a comment (with perhaps spaces before it) is effectively blank, and is ignored.

3.2 What Name to Give Your Makefile

By default, when **make** looks for the makefile, it tries the following names, in order: 'GNUmakefile', 'makefile' and 'Makefile'.

Normally you should call your makefile either 'makefile' or 'Makefile'. (We recommend 'Makefile' because it appears prominently near the beginning of a directory listing, right near other important files such as 'README'.) The first name checked, 'GNUmakefile', is not recommended for most makefiles. You should use this name if you have a makefile that is specific to GNU make, and will not be understood by other versions of make. Other make programs look for 'makefile' and 'Makefile', but not 'GNUmakefile'.

If make finds none of these names, it does not use any makefile. Then you must specify a goal with a command argument, and make will attempt to figure out how to remake it using only its built-in implicit rules. See Chapter 10 [Using Implicit Rules], page 95.

If you want to use a nonstandard name for your makefile, you can specify the makefile name with the '-f' or '--file' option. The arguments '-f name' or '--file=name' tell make to read the file name as the makefile. If you use more than one '-f' or '--file' option, you can specify several makefiles. All the makefiles are effectively concatenated in the order specified. The default makefile names 'GNUmakefile', 'makefile' and 'Makefile' are not checked automatically if you specify '-f' or '--file'.

3.3 Including Other Makefiles

The include directive tells make to suspend reading the current makefile and read one or more other makefiles before continuing. The directive is a line in the makefile that looks like this:

```
include filenames...
```

filenames can contain shell file name patterns.

Extra spaces are allowed and ignored at the beginning of the line, but a tab is not allowed. (If the line begins with a tab, it will be considered a command line.) Whitespace is required between include and the file names, and between file names; extra whitespace is ignored there and at the end of the directive. A comment starting with '#' is allowed at the end of the line. If the file names contain any variable or function references, they are expanded. See Chapter 6 [How to Use Variables], page 51.

For example, if you have three '.mk' files, 'a.mk', 'b.mk', and 'c.mk', and $(bar) expands to bish bash, then the following expression

```
include foo *.mk $(bar)
```

is equivalent to

```
include foo a.mk b.mk c.mk bish bash
```

When make processes an include directive, it suspends reading of the containing makefile and reads from each listed file in turn. When that is finished, make resumes reading the makefile in which the directive appears.

One occasion for using `include` directives is when several programs, handled by individual makefiles in various directories, need to use a common set of variable definitions (see Section 6.5 [Setting Variables], page 58) or pattern rules (see Section 10.5 [Defining and Redefining Pattern Rules], page 103).

Another such occasion is when you want to generate dependencies from source files automatically; the dependencies can be put in a file that is included by the main makefile. This practice is generally cleaner than that of somehow appending the dependencies to the end of the main makefile as has been traditionally done with other versions of **make**. See Section 4.12 [Automatic Dependencies], page 34.

If the specified name does not start with a slash, and the file is not found in the current directory, several other directories are searched. First, any directories you have specified with the '`-I`' or '`--include-dir`' option are searched (see Section 9.7 [Summary of Options], page 89). Then the following directories (if they exist) are searched, in this order: '*prefix*`/include`' (normally '`/usr/local/include`'[1]) '`/usr/gnu/include`', '`/usr/local/include`', '`/usr/include`'.

If an included makefile cannot be found in any of these directories, a warning message is generated, but it is not an immediately fatal error; processing of the makefile containing the `include` continues. Once it has finished reading makefiles, **make** will try to remake any that are out of date or don't exist. See Section 3.5 [How Makefiles Are Remade], page 14. Only after it has tried to find a way to remake a makefile and failed, will **make** diagnose the missing makefile as a fatal error.

If you want **make** to simply ignore a makefile which does not exist and cannot be remade, with no error message, use the `-include` directive instead of `include`, like this:

        -include *filenames*...

This is acts like `include` in every way except that there is no error (not even a warning) if any of the *filenames* do not exist. For compatibility with some other **make** implementations, `sinclude` is another name for `-include`.

3.4 The Variable `MAKEFILES`

If the environment variable `MAKEFILES` is defined, **make** considers its value as a list of names (separated by whitespace) of additional makefiles to be read before the others. This works much like the `include` directive: various directories are searched for those files (see Section 3.3 [Including Other Makefiles], page 12). In addition, the default goal is never taken from one

---

[1] GNU Make compiled for MS-DOS and MS-Windows behaves as if *prefix* has been defined to be the root of the DJGPP tree hierarchy.

of these makefiles and it is not an error if the files listed in MAKEFILES are
not found.

The main use of MAKEFILES is in communication between recursive invocations of make (see Section 5.6 [Recursive Use of make], page 42). It
usually is not desirable to set the environment variable before a top-level
invocation of make, because it is usually better not to mess with a makefile
from outside. However, if you are running make without a specific makefile,
a makefile in MAKEFILES can do useful things to help the built-in implicit
rules work better, such as defining search paths (see Section 4.3 [Directory
Search], page 21).

Some users are tempted to set MAKEFILES in the environment automatically on login, and program makefiles to expect this to be done. This is a
very bad idea, because such makefiles will fail to work if run by anyone else.
It is much better to write explicit include directives in the makefiles. See
Section 3.3 [Including Other Makefiles], page 12.

3.5 How Makefiles Are Remade

Sometimes makefiles can be remade from other files, such as RCS or
SCCS files. If a makefile can be remade from other files, you probably want
make to get an up-to-date version of the makefile to read in.

To this end, after reading in all makefiles, make will consider each as a
goal target and attempt to update it. If a makefile has a rule which says how
to update it (found either in that very makefile or in another one) or if an
implicit rule applies to it (see Chapter 10 [Using Implicit Rules], page 95),
it will be updated if necessary. After all makefiles have been checked, if any
have actually been changed, make starts with a clean slate and reads all the
makefiles over again. (It will also attempt to update each of them over again,
but normally this will not change them again, since they are already up to
date.)

If the makefiles specify a double-colon rule to remake a file with commands but no dependencies, that file will always be remade (see Section 4.11
[Double-Colon], page 34). In the case of makefiles, a makefile that has a
double-colon rule with commands but no dependencies will be remade every time make is run, and then again after make starts over and reads the
makefiles in again. This would cause an infinite loop: make would constantly
remake the makefile, and never do anything else. So, to avoid this, make will
not attempt to remake makefiles which are specified as double-colon targets
but have no dependencies.

If you do not specify any makefiles to be read with '-f' or '--file'
options, make will try the default makefile names; see Section 3.2 [What
Name to Give Your Makefile], page 11. Unlike makefiles explicitly requested
with '-f' or '--file' options, make is not certain that these makefiles should

exist. However, if a default makefile does not exist but can be created by running **make** rules, you probably want the rules to be run so that the makefile can be used.

Therefore, if none of the default makefiles exists, **make** will try to make each of them in the same order in which they are searched for (see Section 3.2 [What Name to Give Your Makefile], page 11) until it succeeds in making one, or it runs out of names to try. Note that it is not an error if **make** cannot find or make any makefile; a makefile is not always necessary.

When you use the '-t' or '--touch' option (see Section 9.3 [Instead of Executing the Commands], page 85), you would not want to use an out-of-date makefile to decide which targets to touch. So the '-t' option has no effect on updating makefiles; they are really updated even if '-t' is specified. Likewise, '-q' (or '--question') and '-n' (or '--just-print') do not prevent updating of makefiles, because an out-of-date makefile would result in the wrong output for other targets. Thus, 'make -f mfile -n foo' will update 'mfile', read it in, and then print the commands to update 'foo' and its dependencies without running them. The commands printed for 'foo' will be those specified in the updated contents of 'mfile'.

However, on occasion you might actually wish to prevent updating of even the makefiles. You can do this by specifying the makefiles as goals in the command line as well as specifying them as makefiles. When the makefile name is specified explicitly as a goal, the options '-t' and so on do apply to them.

Thus, 'make -f mfile -n mfile foo' would read the makefile 'mfile', print the commands needed to update it without actually running them, and then print the commands needed to update 'foo' without running them. The commands for 'foo' will be those specified by the existing contents of 'mfile'.

3.6 Overriding Part of Another Makefile

Sometimes it is useful to have a makefile that is mostly just like another makefile. You can often use the 'include' directive to include one in the other, and add more targets or variable definitions. However, if the two makefiles give different commands for the same target, **make** will not let you just do this. But there is another way.

In the containing makefile (the one that wants to include the other), you can use a match-anything pattern rule to say that to remake any target that cannot be made from the information in the containing makefile, **make** should look in another makefile. See Section 10.5 [Pattern Rules], page 103, for more information on pattern rules.

For example, if you have a makefile called 'Makefile' that says how to make the target 'foo' (and other targets), you can write a makefile called 'GNUmakefile' that contains:

```
foo:
        frobnicate > foo

%: force
        @$(MAKE) -f Makefile $@
force: ;
```

If you say 'make foo', make will find 'GNUmakefile', read it, and see that to make 'foo', it needs to run the command 'frobnicate > foo'. If you say 'make bar', make will find no way to make 'bar' in 'GNUmakefile', so it will use the commands from the pattern rule: 'make -f Makefile bar'. If 'Makefile' provides a rule for updating 'bar', make will apply the rule. And likewise for any other target that 'GNUmakefile' does not say how to make.

The way this works is that the pattern rule has a pattern of just '%', so it matches any target whatever. The rule specifies a dependency 'force', to guarantee that the commands will be run even if the target file already exists. We give 'force' target empty commands to prevent make from searching for an implicit rule to build it—otherwise it would apply the same match-anything rule to 'force' itself and create a dependency loop!

4 Writing Rules

A *rule* appears in the makefile and says when and how to remake certain files, called the rule's *targets* (most often only one per rule). It lists the other files that are the *dependencies* of the target, and *commands* to use to create or update the target.

The order of rules is not significant, except for determining the *default goal*: the target for `make` to consider, if you do not otherwise specify one. The default goal is the target of the first rule in the first makefile. If the first rule has multiple targets, only the first target is taken as the default. There are two exceptions: a target starting with a period is not a default unless it contains one or more slashes, '`/`', as well; and, a target that defines a pattern rule has no effect on the default goal. (See Section 10.5 [Defining and Redefining Pattern Rules], page 103.)

Therefore, we usually write the makefile so that the first rule is the one for compiling the entire program or all the programs described by the makefile (often with a target called '`all`'). See Section 9.2 [Arguments to Specify the Goals], page 83.

4.1 Rule Syntax

In general, a rule looks like this:

```
targets : dependencies
        command
        . . .
```

or like this:

```
targets : dependencies ; command
        command
        . . .
```

The *targets* are file names, separated by spaces. Wildcard characters may be used (see Section 4.2 [Using Wildcard Characters in File Names], page 18) and a name of the form '`a(m)`' represents member *m* in archive file *a* (see Section 11.1 [Archive Members as Targets], page 115). Usually there is only one target per rule, but occasionally there is a reason to have more (see Section 4.8 [Multiple Targets in a Rule], page 30).

The *command* lines start with a tab character. The first command may appear on the line after the dependencies, with a tab character, or may appear on the same line, with a semicolon. Either way, the effect is the same. See Chapter 5 [Writing the Commands in Rules], page 37.

Because dollar signs are used to start variable references, if you really want a dollar sign in a rule you must write two of them, '`$$`' (see Chapter 6 [How to Use Variables], page 51). You may split a long line by inserting a backslash followed by a newline, but this is not required, as make places no limit on the length of a line in a makefile.

A rule tells make two things: when the targets are out of date, and how to update them when necessary.

The criterion for being out of date is specified in terms of the *dependencies*, which consist of file names separated by spaces. (Wildcards and archive members (see Chapter 11 [Archives], page 115) are allowed here too.) A target is out of date if it does not exist or if it is older than any of the dependencies (by comparison of last-modification times). The idea is that the contents of the target file are computed based on information in the dependencies, so if any of the dependencies changes, the contents of the existing target file are no longer necessarily valid.

How to update is specified by *commands*. These are lines to be executed by the shell (normally 'sh'), but with some extra features (see Chapter 5 [Writing the Commands in Rules], page 37).

4.2 Using Wildcard Characters in File Names

A single file name can specify many files using *wildcard characters*. The wildcard characters in make are '*', '?' and '[...]', the same as in the Bourne shell. For example, '*.c' specifies a list of all the files (in the working directory) whose names end in '.c'.

The character '~' at the beginning of a file name also has special significance. If alone, or followed by a slash, it represents your home directory. For example '~/bin' expands to '/home/you/bin'. If the '~' is followed by a word, the string represents the home directory of the user named by that word. For example '~john/bin' expands to '/home/john/bin'. On systems which don't have a home directory for each user (such as MS-DOS or MS-Windows), this functionality can be simulated by setting the environment variable *HOME*.

Wildcard expansion happens automatically in targets, in dependencies, and in commands (where the shell does the expansion). In other contexts, wildcard expansion happens only if you request it explicitly with the wildcard function.

The special significance of a wildcard character can be turned off by preceding it with a backslash. Thus, 'foo*bar' would refer to a specific file whose name consists of 'foo', an asterisk, and 'bar'.

4.2.1 Wildcard Examples

Wildcards can be used in the commands of a rule, where they are expanded by the shell. For example, here is a rule to delete all the object files:

```
clean:
        rm -f *.o
```

Wildcards are also useful in the dependencies of a rule. With the following rule in the makefile, 'make print' will print all the '.c' files that have changed since the last time you printed them:

```
print: *.c
        lpr -p $?
        touch print
```

This rule uses 'print' as an empty target file; see Section 4.6 [Empty Target Files to Record Events], page 27. (The automatic variable '$?' is used to print only those files that have changed; see Section 10.5.3 [Automatic Variables], page 106.)

Wildcard expansion does not happen when you define a variable. Thus, if you write this:

```
objects = *.o
```

then the value of the variable objects is the actual string '*.o'. However, if you use the value of objects in a target, dependency or command, wildcard expansion will take place at that time. To set objects to the expansion, instead use:

```
objects := $(wildcard *.o)
```

See Section 4.2.3 [Wildcard Function], page 20.

4.2.2 Pitfalls of Using Wildcards

Now here is an example of a naive way of using wildcard expansion, that does not do what you would intend. Suppose you would like to say that the executable file 'foo' is made from all the object files in the directory, and you write this:

```
objects = *.o

foo : $(objects)
        cc -o foo $(CFLAGS) $(objects)
```

The value of objects is the actual string '*.o'. Wildcard expansion happens in the rule for 'foo', so that each *existing* '.o' file becomes a dependency of 'foo' and will be recompiled if necessary.

But what if you delete all the '.o' files? When a wildcard matches no files, it is left as it is, so then 'foo' will depend on the oddly-named file '*.o'. Since no such file is likely to exist, make will give you an error saying it cannot figure out how to make '*.o'. This is not what you want!

Actually it is possible to obtain the desired result with wildcard expansion, but you need more sophisticated techniques, including the wildcard function and string substitution. These are described in the following section.

Microsoft operating systems (MS-DOS and MS-Windows) use backslashes to separate directories in pathnames, like so:

```
c:\foo\bar\baz.c
```

This is equivalent to the Unix-style 'c:/foo/bar/baz.c' (the 'c:' part is the so-called drive letter). When make runs on these systems, it supports backslashes as well as the Unix-style forward slashes in pathnames. However, this support does *not* include the wildcard expansion, where backslash is a quote character. Therefore, you *must* use Unix-style slashes in these cases.

4.2.3 The Function wildcard

Wildcard expansion happens automatically in rules. But wildcard expansion does not normally take place when a variable is set, or inside the arguments of a function. If you want to do wildcard expansion in such places, you need to use the wildcard function, like this:

```
$(wildcard pattern...)
```

This string, used anywhere in a makefile, is replaced by a space-separated list of names of existing files that match one of the given file name patterns. If no existing file name matches a pattern, then that pattern is omitted from the output of the wildcard function. Note that this is different from how unmatched wildcards behave in rules, where they are used verbatim rather than ignored (see Section 4.2.2 [Wildcard Pitfall], page 19).

One use of the wildcard function is to get a list of all the C source files in a directory, like this:

```
$(wildcard *.c)
```

We can change the list of C source files into a list of object files by replacing the '.c' suffix with '.o' in the result, like this:

```
$(patsubst %.c,%.o,$(wildcard *.c))
```

(Here we have used another function, patsubst. See Section 8.2 [Functions for String Substitution and Analysis], page 72.)

Thus, a makefile to compile all C source files in the directory and then link them together could be written as follows:

```
objects := $(patsubst %.c,%.o,$(wildcard *.c))

foo : $(objects)
        cc -o foo $(objects)
```

(This takes advantage of the implicit rule for compiling C programs, so there is no need to write explicit rules for compiling the files. See Section 6.2 [The Two Flavors of Variables], page 52, for an explanation of ':=', which is a variant of '='.)

4.3 Searching Directories for Dependencies

For large systems, it is often desirable to put sources in a separate directory from the binaries. The *directory search* features of `make` facilitate this by searching several directories automatically to find a dependency. When you redistribute the files among directories, you do not need to change the individual rules, just the search paths.

4.3.1 `VPATH`: Search Path for All Dependencies

The value of the `make` variable `VPATH` specifies a list of directories that `make` should search. Most often, the directories are expected to contain dependency files that are not in the current directory; however, `VPATH` specifies a search list that `make` applies for all files, including files which are targets of rules.

Thus, if a file that is listed as a target or dependency does not exist in the current directory, `make` searches the directories listed in `VPATH` for a file with that name. If a file is found in one of them, that file may become the dependency (see below). Rules may then specify the names of files in the dependency list as if they all existed in the current directory. See Section 4.3.4 [Writing Shell Commands with Directory Search], page 24.

In the `VPATH` variable, directory names are separated by colons or blanks. The order in which directories are listed is the order followed by `make` in its search. (On MS-DOS and MS-Windows, semi-colons are used as separators of directory names in `VPATH`, since the colon can be used in the pathname itself, after the drive letter.)

For example,

```
VPATH = src:../headers
```

specifies a path containing two directories, 'src' and '../headers', which `make` searches in that order.

With this value of `VPATH`, the following rule,

```
foo.o : foo.c
```

is interpreted as if it were written like this:

```
foo.o : src/foo.c
```

assuming the file 'foo.c' does not exist in the current directory but is found in the directory 'src'.

4.3.2 The `vpath` Directive

Similar to the `VPATH` variable, but more selective, is the `vpath` directive (note lower case), which allows you to specify a search path for a particular class of file names: those that match a particular pattern. Thus you can supply certain search directories for one class of file names and other directories (or none) for other file names.

There are three forms of the vpath directive:

vpath *pattern directories*

> Specify the search path *directories* for file names that match *pattern*.

> The search path, *directories*, is a list of directories to be searched, separated by colons (semi-colons on MS-DOS and MS-Windows) or blanks, just like the search path used in the VPATH variable.

vpath *pattern*

> Clear out the search path associated with *pattern*.

vpath

> Clear all search paths previously specified with vpath directives.

A vpath pattern is a string containing a '%' character. The string must match the file name of a dependency that is being searched for, the '%' character matching any sequence of zero or more characters (as in pattern rules; see Section 10.5 [Defining and Redefining Pattern Rules], page 103). For example, %.h matches files that end in .h. (If there is no '%', the pattern must match the dependency exactly, which is not useful very often.)

'%' characters in a vpath directive's pattern can be quoted with preceding backslashes ('\'). Backslashes that would otherwise quote '%' characters can be quoted with more backslashes. Backslashes that quote '%' characters or other backslashes are removed from the pattern before it is compared to file names. Backslashes that are not in danger of quoting '%' characters go unmolested.

When a dependency fails to exist in the current directory, if the *pattern* in a vpath directive matches the name of the dependency file, then the *directories* in that directive are searched just like (and before) the directories in the VPATH variable.

For example,

```
vpath %.h ../headers
```

tells make to look for any dependency whose name ends in '.h' in the directory '../headers' if the file is not found in the current directory.

If several vpath patterns match the dependency file's name, then make processes each matching vpath directive one by one, searching all the directories mentioned in each directive. make handles multiple vpath directives in the order in which they appear in the makefile; multiple directives with the same pattern are independent of each other.

Thus,

```
vpath %.c foo
vpath %   blish
vpath %.c bar
```

will look for a file ending in '.c' in 'foo', then 'blish', then 'bar', while

```
vpath %.c foo:bar
vpath %   blish
```

will look for a file ending in '.c' in 'foo', then 'bar', then 'blish'.

4.3.3 How Directory Searches are Performed

When a dependency is found through directory search, regardless of type (general or selective), the pathname located may not be the one that make actually provides you in the dependency list. Sometimes the path discovered through directory search is thrown away.

The algorithm make uses to decide whether to keep or abandon a path found via directory search is as follows:

1. If a target file does not exist at the path specified in the makefile, directory search is performed.

2. If the directory search is successful, that path is kept and this file is tentatively stored as the target.

3. All dependencies of this target are examined using this same method.

4. After processing the dependencies, the target may or may not need to be rebuilt:

   a. If the target does *not* need to be rebuilt, the path to the file found during directory search is used for any dependency lists which contain this target. In short, if make doesn't need to rebuild the target then you use the path found via directory search.

   b. If the target *does* need to be rebuilt (is out-of-date), the pathname found during directory search is *thrown away*, and the target is rebuilt using the file name specified in the makefile. In short, if make must rebuild, then the target is rebuilt locally, not in the directory found via directory search.

This algorithm may seem complex, but in practice it is quite often exactly what you want.

Other versions of make use a simpler algorithm: if the file does not exist, and it is found via directory search, then that pathname is always used whether or not the target needs to be built. Thus, if the target is rebuilt it is created at the pathname discovered during directory search.

If, in fact, this is the behavior you want for some or all of your directories, you can use the GPATH variable to indicate this to make.

GPATH has the same syntax and format as VPATH (that is, a space- or colon-delimited list of pathnames). If an out-of-date target is found by directory search in a directory that also appears in GPATH, then that pathname is not thrown away. The target is rebuilt using the expanded path.

4.3.4 Writing Shell Commands with Directory Search

When a dependency is found in another directory through directory search, this cannot change the commands of the rule; they will execute as written. Therefore, you must write the commands with care so that they will look for the dependency in the directory where make finds it.

This is done with the *automatic variables* such as '$^' (see Section 10.5.3 [Automatic Variables], page 106). For instance, the value of '$^' is a list of all the dependencies of the rule, including the names of the directories in which they were found, and the value of '$@' is the target. Thus:

```
foo.o : foo.c
        cc -c $(CFLAGS) $^ -o $@
```

(The variable CFLAGS exists so you can specify flags for C compilation by implicit rules; we use it here for consistency so it will affect all C compilations uniformly; see Section 10.3 [Variables Used by Implicit Rules], page 100.)

Often the dependencies include header files as well, which you do not want to mention in the commands. The automatic variable '$<' is just the first dependency:

```
VPATH = src:../headers
foo.o : foo.c defs.h hack.h
        cc -c $(CFLAGS) $< -o $@
```

4.3.5 Directory Search and Implicit Rules

The search through the directories specified in VPATH or with vpath also happens during consideration of implicit rules (see Chapter 10 [Using Implicit Rules], page 95).

For example, when a file 'foo.o' has no explicit rule, make considers implicit rules, such as the built-in rule to compile 'foo.c' if that file exists. If such a file is lacking in the current directory, the appropriate directories are searched for it. If 'foo.c' exists (or is mentioned in the makefile) in any of the directories, the implicit rule for C compilation is applied.

The commands of implicit rules normally use automatic variables as a matter of necessity; consequently they will use the file names found by directory search with no extra effort.

4.3.6 Directory Search for Link Libraries

Directory search applies in a special way to libraries used with the linker. This special feature comes into play when you write a dependency whose name is of the form '-l*name*'. (You can tell something strange is going on here because the dependency is normally the name of a file, and the *file name* of the library looks like 'lib*name*.a', not like '-l*name*'.)

When a dependency's name has the form '-l*name*', make handles it specially by searching for the file 'lib*name*.a' in the current directory, in directories specified by matching vpath search paths and the VPATH search path, and then in the directories '/lib', '/usr/lib', and '*prefix*/lib' (normally '/usr/local/lib', but MS-DOS/MS-Windows versions of make behave as if *prefix* is defined to be the root of the DJGPP installation tree).

For example,

```
foo : foo.c -lcurses
        cc $^ -o $@
```

would cause the command 'cc foo.c /usr/lib/libcurses.a -o foo' to be executed when 'foo' is older than 'foo.c' or than '/usr/lib/libcurses.a'.

4.4 Phony Targets

A phony target is one that is not really the name of a file. It is just a name for some commands to be executed when you make an explicit request. There are two reasons to use a phony target: to avoid a conflict with a file of the same name, and to improve performance.

If you write a rule whose commands will not create the target file, the commands will be executed every time the target comes up for remaking. Here is an example:

```
clean:
        rm *.o temp
```

Because the rm command does not create a file named 'clean', probably no such file will ever exist. Therefore, the rm command will be executed every time you say 'make clean'.

The phony target will cease to work if anything ever does create a file named 'clean' in this directory. Since it has no dependencies, the file 'clean' would inevitably be considered up to date, and its commands would not be executed. To avoid this problem, you can explicitly declare the target to be phony, using the special target .PHONY (see Section 4.7 [Special Built-in Target Names], page 28) as follows:

```
.PHONY : clean
```

Once this is done, 'make clean' will run the commands regardless of whether there is a file named 'clean'.

Since it knows that phony targets do not name actual files that could be remade from other files, make skips the implicit rule search for phony targets (see Chapter 10 [Implicit Rules], page 95). This is why declaring a target phony is good for performance, even if you are not worried about the actual file existing.

Thus, you first write the line that states that clean is a phony target, then you write the rule, like this:

```
.PHONY: clean
clean:
        rm *.o temp
```

A phony target should not be a dependency of a real target file; if it is, its commands are run every time make goes to update that file. As long as a phony target is never a dependency of a real target, the phony target commands will be executed only when the phony target is a specified goal (see Section 9.2 [Arguments to Specify the Goals], page 83).

Phony targets can have dependencies. When one directory contains multiple programs, it is most convenient to describe all of the programs in one makefile './Makefile'. Since the target remade by default will be the first one in the makefile, it is common to make this a phony target named 'all' and give it, as dependencies, all the individual programs. For example:

```
all : prog1 prog2 prog3
.PHONY : all

prog1 : prog1.o utils.o
        cc -o prog1 prog1.o utils.o

prog2 : prog2.o
        cc -o prog2 prog2.o

prog3 : prog3.o sort.o utils.o
        cc -o prog3 prog3.o sort.o utils.o
```

Now you can say just 'make' to remake all three programs, or specify as arguments the ones to remake (as in 'make prog1 prog3').

When one phony target is a dependency of another, it serves as a subroutine of the other. For example, here 'make cleanall' will delete the object files, the difference files, and the file 'program':

```
.PHONY: cleanall cleanobj cleandiff

cleanall : cleanobj cleandiff
        rm program

cleanobj :
```

```
        rm *.o

cleandiff :
        rm *.diff
```

4.5 Rules without Commands or Dependencies

If a rule has no dependencies or commands, and the target of the rule is a nonexistent file, then **make** imagines this target to have been updated whenever its rule is run. This implies that all targets depending on this one will always have their commands run.

An example will illustrate this:

```
clean: FORCE
        rm $(objects)
FORCE:
```

Here the target 'FORCE' satisfies the special conditions, so the target 'clean' that depends on it is forced to run its commands. There is nothing special about the name 'FORCE', but that is one name commonly used this way.

As you can see, using 'FORCE' this way has the same results as using '.PHONY: clean'.

Using '.PHONY' is more explicit and more efficient. However, other versions of **make** do not support '.PHONY'; thus 'FORCE' appears in many makefiles. See Section 4.4 [Phony Targets], page 25.

4.6 Empty Target Files to Record Events

The *empty target* is a variant of the phony target; it is used to hold commands for an action that you request explicitly from time to time. Unlike a phony target, this target file can really exist; but the file's contents do not matter, and usually are empty.

The purpose of the empty target file is to record, with its last-modification time, when the rule's commands were last executed. It does so because one of the commands is a **touch** command to update the target file.

The empty target file must have some dependencies. When you ask to remake the empty target, the commands are executed if any dependency is more recent than the target; in other words, if a dependency has changed since the last time you remade the target. Here is an example:

```
print: foo.c bar.c
        lpr -p $?
        touch print
```

With this rule, 'make print' will execute the lpr command if either source file has changed since the last 'make print'. The automatic variable '$?' is used to print only those files that have changed (see Section 10.5.3 [Automatic Variables], page 106).

4.7 Special Built-in Target Names

Certain names have special meanings if they appear as targets.

.PHONY

> The dependencies of the special target .PHONY are considered to be phony targets. When it is time to consider such a target, make will run its commands unconditionally, regardless of whether a file with that name exists or what its last-modification time is. See Section 4.4 [Phony Targets], page 25.

.SUFFIXES

> The dependencies of the special target .SUFFIXES are the list of suffixes to be used in checking for suffix rules. See Section 10.7 [Old-Fashioned Suffix Rules], page 111.

.DEFAULT

> The commands specified for .DEFAULT are used for any target for which no rules are found (either explicit rules or implicit rules). See Section 10.6 [Last Resort], page 110. If .DEFAULT commands are specified, every file mentioned as a dependency, but not as a target in a rule, will have these commands executed on its behalf. See Section 10.8 [Implicit Rule Search Algorithm], page 112.

.PRECIOUS

> The targets which .PRECIOUS depends on are given the following special treatment: if make is killed or interrupted during the execution of their commands, the target is not deleted. See Section 5.5 [Interrupting or Killing make], page 42. Also, if the target is an intermediate file, it will not be deleted after it is no longer needed, as is normally done. See Section 10.4 [Chains of Implicit Rules], page 102.

> You can also list the target pattern of an implicit rule (such as '%.o') as a dependency file of the special target .PRECIOUS to preserve intermediate files created by rules whose target patterns match that file's name.

.INTERMEDIATE

> The targets which .INTERMEDIATE depends on are treated as intermediate files. See Section 10.4 [Chains of Implicit Rules],

page 102. `.INTERMEDIATE` with no dependencies marks all file targets mentioned in the makefile as intermediate.

`.SECONDARY`

The targets which `.SECONDARY` depends on are treated as intermediate files, except that they are never automatically deleted. See Section 10.4 [Chains of Implicit Rules], page 102.

`.SECONDARY` with no dependencies marks all file targets mentioned in the makefile as secondary.

`.IGNORE`

If you specify dependencies for `.IGNORE`, then make will ignore errors in execution of the commands run for those particular files. The commands for `.IGNORE` are not meaningful.

If mentioned as a target with no dependencies, `.IGNORE` says to ignore errors in execution of commands for all files. This usage of '`.IGNORE`' is supported only for historical compatibility. Since this affects every command in the makefile, it is not very useful; we recommend you use the more selective ways to ignore errors in specific commands. See Section 5.4 [Errors in Commands], page 40.

`.SILENT`

If you specify dependencies for `.SILENT`, then make will not the print commands to remake those particular files before executing them. The commands for `.SILENT` are not meaningful.

If mentioned as a target with no dependencies, `.SILENT` says not to print any commands before executing them. This usage of '`.SILENT`' is supported only for historical compatibility. We recommend you use the more selective ways to silence specific commands. See Section 5.1 [Command Echoing], page 37. If you want to silence all commands for a particular run of make, use the '`-s`' or '`--silent`' option (see Section 9.7 [Options Summary], page 89).

`.EXPORT_ALL_VARIABLES`

Simply by being mentioned as a target, this tells make to export all variables to child processes by default. See Section 5.6.2 [Communicating Variables to a Sub-make], page 44.

Any defined implicit rule suffix also counts as a special target if it appears as a target, and so does the concatenation of two suffixes, such as '`.c.o`'. These targets are suffix rules, an obsolete way of defining implicit rules (but a way still widely used). In principle, any target name could be special in this way if you break it in two and add both pieces to the suffix list. In practice, suffixes normally begin with '`.`', so these special target names also begin with '`.`'. See Section 10.7 [Old-Fashioned Suffix Rules], page 111.

4.8 Multiple Targets in a Rule

A rule with multiple targets is equivalent to writing many rules, each with
one target, and all identical aside from that. The same commands apply to
all the targets, but their effects may vary because you can substitute the
actual target name into the command using '$@'. The rule contributes the
same dependencies to all the targets also.

This is useful in two cases.

- You want just dependencies, no commands. For example:

    ```
    kbd.o command.o files.o: command.h
    ```

    gives an additional dependency to each of the three object files men-
    tioned.

- Similar commands work for all the targets. The commands do not need
  to be absolutely identical, since the automatic variable '$@' can be used
  to substitute the particular target to be remade into the commands (see
  Section 10.5.3 [Automatic Variables], page 106). For example:

    ```
    bigoutput littleoutput : text.g
            generate text.g -$(subst output,,$@) > $@
    ```

    is equivalent to

    ```
    bigoutput : text.g
            generate text.g -big > bigoutput
    littleoutput : text.g
            generate text.g -little > littleoutput
    ```

    Here we assume the hypothetical program generate makes two types of
    output, one if given '-big' and one if given '-little'. See Section 8.2
    [Functions for String Substitution and Analysis], page 72, for an expla-
    nation of the subst function.

Suppose you would like to vary the dependencies according to the target,
much as the variable '$@' allows you to vary the commands. You cannot do
this with multiple targets in an ordinary rule, but you can do it with a *static
pattern rule*. See Section 4.10 [Static Pattern Rules], page 31.

4.9 Multiple Rules for One Target

One file can be the target of several rules. All the dependencies mentioned
in all the rules are merged into one list of dependencies for the target. If
the target is older than any dependency from any rule, the commands are
executed.

There can only be one set of commands to be executed for a file. If
more than one rule gives commands for the same file, make uses the last
set given and prints an error message. (As a special case, if the file's name
begins with a dot, no error message is printed. This odd behavior is only for

compatibility with other implementations of `make`.) There is no reason to write your makefiles this way; that is why `make` gives you an error message.

An extra rule with just dependencies can be used to give a few extra dependencies to many files at once. For example, one usually has a variable named `objects` containing a list of all the compiler output files in the system being made. An easy way to say that all of them must be recompiled if 'config.h' changes is to write the following:

```
objects = foo.o bar.o
foo.o : defs.h
bar.o : defs.h test.h
$(objects) : config.h
```

This could be inserted or taken out without changing the rules that really specify how to make the object files, making it a convenient form to use if you wish to add the additional dependency intermittently.

Another wrinkle is that the additional dependencies could be specified with a variable that you set with a command argument to `make` (see Section 9.5 [Overriding Variables], page 87). For example,

```
extradeps=
$(objects) : $(extradeps)
```

means that the command 'make extradeps=foo.h' will consider 'foo.h' as a dependency of each object file, but plain 'make' will not.

If none of the explicit rules for a target has commands, then `make` searches for an applicable implicit rule to find some commands see Chapter 10 [Using Implicit Rules], page 95).

4.10 Static Pattern Rules

Static pattern rules are rules which specify multiple targets and construct the dependency names for each target based on the target name. They are more general than ordinary rules with multiple targets because the targets do not have to have identical dependencies. Their dependencies must be *analogous*, but not necessarily *identical*.

4.10.1 Syntax of Static Pattern Rules

Here is the syntax of a static pattern rule:

```
targets ...: target-pattern: dep-patterns ...
        commands

        ...
```

The *targets* list specifies the targets that the rule applies to. The targets can contain wildcard characters, just like the targets of ordinary rules (see Section 4.2 [Using Wildcard Characters in File Names], page 18).

The *target-pattern* and *dep-patterns* say how to compute the dependencies of each target. Each target is matched against the *target-pattern* to extract a part of the target name, called the *stem*. This stem is substituted into each of the *dep-patterns* to make the dependency names (one from each *dep-pattern*).

Each pattern normally contains the character '%' just once. When the *target-pattern* matches a target, the '%' can match any part of the target name; this part is called the *stem*. The rest of the pattern must match exactly. For example, the target 'foo.o' matches the pattern '%.o', with 'foo' as the stem. The targets 'foo.c' and 'foo.out' do not match that pattern.

The dependency names for each target are made by substituting the stem for the '%' in each dependency pattern. For example, if one dependency pattern is '%.c', then substitution of the stem 'foo' gives the dependency name 'foo.c'. It is legitimate to write a dependency pattern that does not contain '%'; then this dependency is the same for all targets.

'%' characters in pattern rules can be quoted with preceding backslashes ('\'). Backslashes that would otherwise quote '%' characters can be quoted with more backslashes. Backslashes that quote '%' characters or other backslashes are removed from the pattern before it is compared to file names or has a stem substituted into it. Backslashes that are not in danger of quoting '%' characters go unmolested. For example, the pattern 'the\%weird\\%pattern\\' has 'the%weird\' preceding the operative '%' character, and 'pattern\\' following it. The final two backslashes are left alone because they cannot affect any '%' character.

Here is an example, which compiles each of 'foo.o' and 'bar.o' from the corresponding '.c' file:

```
objects = foo.o bar.o

all: $(objects)

$(objects): %.o: %.c
        $(CC) -c $(CFLAGS) $< -o $@
```

Here '$<' is the automatic variable that holds the name of the dependency and '$@' is the automatic variable that holds the name of the target; see Section 10.5.3 [Automatic Variables], page 106.

Each target specified must match the target pattern; a warning is issued for each target that does not. If you have a list of files, only some of which will match the pattern, you can use the **filter** function to remove nonmatching file names (see Section 8.2 [Functions for String Substitution and Analysis], page 72):

```
files = foo.elc bar.o lose.o
```

```
$(filter %.o,$(files)): %.o: %.c
        $(CC) -c $(CFLAGS) $< -o $@
$(filter %.elc,$(files)): %.elc: %.el
        emacs -f batch-byte-compile $<
```

In this example the result of '$(filter %.o,$(files))' is 'bar.o lose.o', and the first static pattern rule causes each of these object files to be updated by compiling the corresponding C source file. The result of '$(filter %.elc,$(files))' is 'foo.elc', so that file is made from 'foo.el'.

Another example shows how to use $* in static pattern rules:

```
bigoutput littleoutput : %output : text.g
        generate text.g -$* > $@
```

When the generate command is run, $* will expand to the stem, either 'big' or 'little'.

4.10.2 Static Pattern Rules versus Implicit Rules

A static pattern rule has much in common with an implicit rule defined as a pattern rule (see Section 10.5 [Defining and Redefining Pattern Rules], page 103). Both have a pattern for the target and patterns for constructing the names of dependencies. The difference is in how make decides *when* the rule applies.

An implicit rule *can* apply to any target that matches its pattern, but it *does* apply only when the target has no commands otherwise specified, and only when the dependencies can be found. If more than one implicit rule appears applicable, only one applies; the choice depends on the order of rules.

By contrast, a static pattern rule applies to the precise list of targets that you specify in the rule. It cannot apply to any other target and it invariably does apply to each of the targets specified. If two conflicting rules apply, and both have commands, that's an error.

The static pattern rule can be better than an implicit rule for these reasons:

- You may wish to override the usual implicit rule for a few files whose names cannot be categorized syntactically but can be given in an explicit list.

- If you cannot be sure of the precise contents of the directories you are using, you may not be sure which other irrelevant files might lead make to use the wrong implicit rule. The choice might depend on the order in which the implicit rule search is done. With static pattern rules, there is no uncertainty: each rule applies to precisely the targets specified.

4.11 Double-Colon Rules

Double-colon rules are rules written with ':' instead of ':' after the target names. They are handled differently from ordinary rules when the same target appears in more than one rule.

When a target appears in multiple rules, all the rules must be the same type: all ordinary, or all double-colon. If they are double-colon, each of them is independent of the others. Each double-colon rule's commands are executed if the target is older than any dependencies of that rule. This can result in executing none, any, or all of the double-colon rules.

Double-colon rules with the same target are in fact completely separate from one another. Each double-colon rule is processed individually, just as rules with different targets are processed.

The double-colon rules for a target are executed in the order they appear in the makefile. However, the cases where double-colon rules really make sense are those where the order of executing the commands would not matter.

Double-colon rules are somewhat obscure and not often very useful; they provide a mechanism for cases in which the method used to update a target differs depending on which dependency files caused the update, and such cases are rare.

Each double-colon rule should specify commands; if it does not, an implicit rule will be used if one applies. See Chapter 10 [Using Implicit Rules], page 95.

4.12 Generating Dependencies Automatically

In the makefile for a program, many of the rules you need to write often say only that some object file depends on some header file. For example, if 'main.c' uses 'defs.h' via an #include, you would write:

```
main.o: defs.h
```

You need this rule so that make knows that it must remake 'main.o' whenever 'defs.h' changes. You can see that for a large program you would have to write dozens of such rules in your makefile. And, you must always be very careful to update the makefile every time you add or remove an #include.

To avoid this hassle, most modern C compilers can write these rules for you, by looking at the #include lines in the source files. Usually this is done with the '-M' option to the compiler. For example, the command:

```
cc -M main.c
```

generates the output:

```
main.o : main.c defs.h
```

Thus you no longer have to write all those rules yourself. The compiler will do it for you.

Note that such a dependency constitutes mentioning 'main.o' in a make-file, so it can never be considered an intermediate file by implicit rule search. This means that make won't ever remove the file after using it; see Section 10.4 [Chains of Implicit Rules], page 102.

With old make programs, it was traditional practice to use this compiler feature to generate dependencies on demand with a command like 'make depend'. That command would create a file 'depend' containing all the automatically-generated dependencies; then the makefile could use include to read them in (see Section 3.3 [Include], page 12).

In GNU make, the feature of remaking makefiles makes this practice obsolete—you need never tell make explicitly to regenerate the dependen-cies, because it always regenerates any makefile that is out of date. See Section 3.5 [Remaking Makefiles], page 14.

The practice we recommend for automatic dependency generation is to have one makefile corresponding to each source file. For each source file 'name.c' there is a makefile 'name.d' which lists what files the object file 'name.o' depends on. That way only the source files that have changed need to be rescanned to produce the new dependencies.

Here is the pattern rule to generate a file of dependencies (i.e., a makefile) called 'name.d' from a C source file called 'name.c':

```
%.d: %.c
        $(SHELL) -ec '$(CC) -M $(CPPFLAGS) $< \
                | sed '\''s/\($*\)\.o[ :]*/\1.o $@ : /g'\'' > $@; \
                [ -s $@ ] || rm -f $@'
```

See Section 10.5 [Pattern Rules], page 103, for information on defining pat-tern rules. The '-e' flag to the shell makes it exit immediately if the $(CC) command fails (exits with a nonzero status). Normally the shell exits with the status of the last command in the pipeline (sed in this case), so make would not notice a nonzero status from the compiler.

With the GNU C compiler, you may wish to use the '-MM' flag instead of '-M'. This omits dependencies on system header files. See section "Options Controlling the Preprocessor" in *Using GNU CC*, for details.

The purpose of the sed command is to translate (for example):

```
main.o : main.c defs.h
```

into:

```
main.o main.d : main.c defs.h
```

This makes each '.d' file depend on all the source and header files that the corresponding '.o' file depends on. make then knows it must regenerate the dependencies whenever any of the source or header files changes.

Once you've defined the rule to remake the '.d' files, you then use the include directive to read them all in. See Section 3.3 [Include], page 12. For example:

```
sources = foo.c bar.c

include $(sources:.c=.d)
```

(This example uses a substitution variable reference to translate the list of source files 'foo.c bar.c' into a list of dependency makefiles, 'foo.d bar.d'. See Section 6.3.1 [Substitution Refs], page 55, for full information on substitution references.) Since the '.d' files are makefiles like any others, make will remake them as necessary with no further work from you. See Section 3.5 [Remaking Makefiles], page 14.

5 Writing the Commands in Rules

The commands of a rule consist of shell command lines to be executed one by one. Each command line must start with a tab, except that the first command line may be attached to the target-and-dependencies line with a semicolon in between. Blank lines and lines of just comments may appear among the command lines; they are ignored. (But beware, an apparently "blank" line that begins with a tab is *not* blank! It is an empty command; see Section 5.8 [Empty Commands], page 49.)

Users use many different shell programs, but commands in makefiles are always interpreted by '/bin/sh' unless the makefile specifies otherwise. See Section 5.2 [Command Execution], page 38.

The shell that is in use determines whether comments can be written on command lines, and what syntax they use. When the shell is '/bin/sh', a '#' starts a comment that extends to the end of the line. The '#' does not have to be at the beginning of a line. Text on a line before a '#' is not part of the comment.

5.1 Command Echoing

Normally **make** prints each command line before it is executed. We call this *echoing* because it gives the appearance that you are typing the commands yourself.

When a line starts with '@', the echoing of that line is suppressed. The '@' is discarded before the command is passed to the shell. Typically you would use this for a command whose only effect is to print something, such as an **echo** command to indicate progress through the makefile:

```
@echo About to make distribution files
```

When **make** is given the flag '-n' or '--just-print', echoing is all that happens, no execution. See Section 9.7 [Summary of Options], page 89. In this case and only this case, even the commands starting with '@' are printed. This flag is useful for finding out which commands **make** thinks are necessary without actually doing them.

The '-s' or '--silent' flag to **make** prevents all echoing, as if all commands started with '@'. A rule in the makefile for the special target .SILENT without dependencies has the same effect (see Section 4.7 [Special Built-in Target Names], page 28). .SILENT is essentially obsolete since '@' is more flexible.

5.2 Command Execution

When it is time to execute commands to update a target, they are executed by making a new subshell for each line. (In practice, make may take shortcuts that do not affect the results.)

Please note: this implies that shell commands such as cd that set variables local to each process will not affect the following command lines.[1] If you want to use cd to affect the next command, put the two on a single line with a semicolon between them. Then make will consider them a single command and pass them, together, to a shell which will execute them in sequence. For example:

```
foo : bar/lose
        cd bar; gobble lose > ../foo
```

If you would like to split a single shell command into multiple lines of text, you must use a backslash at the end of all but the last subline. Such a sequence of lines is combined into a single line, by deleting the backslash-newline sequences, before passing it to the shell. Thus, the following is equivalent to the preceding example:

```
foo : bar/lose
        cd bar; \
        gobble lose > ../foo
```

The program used as the shell is taken from the variable SHELL. By default, the program '/bin/sh' is used.

On MS-DOS, if SHELL is not set, the value of the variable COMSPEC (which is always set) is used instead.

The processing of lines that set the variable SHELL in Makefiles is different on MS-DOS. The stock shell, 'command.com', is ridiculously limited in its functionality and many users of make tend to install a replacement shell. Therefore, on MS-DOS, make examines the value of SHELL, and changes its behavior based on whether it points to a Unix-style or DOS-style shell. This allows reasonable functionality even if SHELL points to 'command.com'.

If SHELL points to a Unix-style shell, make on MS-DOS additionally checks whether that shell can indeed be found; if not, it ignores the line that sets SHELL. In MS-DOS, GNU make searches for the shell in the following places:

1. In the precise place pointed to by the value of SHELL. For example, if the makefile specifies 'SHELL = /bin/sh', make will look in the directory '/bin' on the current drive.

2. In the current directory.

3. In each of the directories in the PATH variable, in order.

---

[1] On MS-DOS, the value of current working directory is **global**, so changing it *will* affect the following command lines on those systems.

In every directory it examines, `make` will first look for the specific file ('sh' in the example above). If this is not found, it will also look in that directory for that file with one of the known extensions which identify executable files. For example '.exe', '.com', '.bat', '.btm', '.sh', and some others.

If any of these attempts is successful, the value of SHELL will be set to the full pathname of the shell as found. However, if none of these is found, the value of SHELL will not be changed, and thus the line that sets it will be effectively ignored. This is so `make` will only support features specific to a Unix-style shell if such a shell is actually installed on the system where `make` runs.

Note that this extended search for the shell is limited to the cases where SHELL is set from the Makefile; if it is set in the environment or command line, you are expected to set it to the full pathname of the shell, exactly as things are on Unix.

The effect of the above DOS-specific processing is that a Makefile that says 'SHELL = /bin/sh' (as many Unix makefiles do), will work on MS-DOS unaltered if you have e.g. 'sh.exe' installed in some directory along your PATH.

Unlike most variables, the variable SHELL is never set from the environment. This is because the SHELL environment variable is used to specify your personal choice of shell program for interactive use. It would be very bad for personal choices like this to affect the functioning of makefiles. See Section 6.9 [Variables from the Environment], page 62. However, on MS-DOS and MS-Windows the value of SHELL in the environment **is** used, since on those systems most users do not set this variable, and therefore it is most likely set specifically to be used by `make`. On MS-DOS, if the setting of SHELL is not suitable for `make`, you can set the variable MAKESHELL to the shell that `make` should use; this will override the value of SHELL.

5.3 Parallel Execution

GNU `make` knows how to execute several commands at once. Normally, `make` will execute only one command at a time, waiting for it to finish before executing the next. However, the '-j' or '--jobs' option tells `make` to execute many commands simultaneously.

On MS-DOS, the '-j' option has no effect, since that system doesn't support multi-processing.

If the '-j' option is followed by an integer, this is the number of commands to execute at once; this is called the number of *job slots*. If there is nothing looking like an integer after the '-j' option, there is no limit on the number of job slots. The default number of job slots is one, which means serial execution (one thing at a time).

One unpleasant consequence of running several commands simultaneously is that output from all of the commands comes when the commands send it, so messages from different commands may be interspersed.

Another problem is that two processes cannot both take input from the same device; so to make sure that only one command tries to take input from the terminal at once, `make` will invalidate the standard input streams of all but one running command. This means that attempting to read from standard input will usually be a fatal error (a '`Broken pipe`' signal) for most child processes if there are several.

It is unpredictable which command will have a valid standard input stream (which will come from the terminal, or wherever you redirect the standard input of `make`). The first command run will always get it first, and the first command started after that one finishes will get it next, and so on.

We will change how this aspect of `make` works if we find a better alternative. In the mean time, you should not rely on any command using standard input at all if you are using the parallel execution feature; but if you are not using this feature, then standard input works normally in all commands.

If a command fails (is killed by a signal or exits with a nonzero status), and errors are not ignored for that command (see Section 5.4 [Errors in Commands], page 40), the remaining command lines to remake the same target will not be run. If a command fails and the '`-k`' or '`--keep-going`' option was not given (see Section 9.7 [Summary of Options], page 89), `make` aborts execution. If make terminates for any reason (including a signal) with child processes running, it waits for them to finish before actually exiting.

When the system is heavily loaded, you will probably want to run fewer jobs than when it is lightly loaded. You can use the '`-l`' option to tell `make` to limit the number of jobs to run at once, based on the load average. The '`-l`' or '`--max-load`' option is followed by a floating-point number. For example,

        -l 2.5

will not let `make` start more than one job if the load average is above 2.5. The '`-l`' option with no following number removes the load limit, if one was given with a previous '`-l`' option.

More precisely, when `make` goes to start up a job, and it already has at least one job running, it checks the current load average; if it is not lower than the limit given with '`-l`', `make` waits until the load average goes below that limit, or until all the other jobs finish.

By default, there is no load limit.

5.4 Errors in Commands

After each shell command returns, `make` looks at its exit status. If the command completed successfully, the next command line is executed in a new shell; after the last command line is finished, the rule is finished.

If there is an error (the exit status is nonzero), `make` gives up on the current rule, and perhaps on all rules.

Sometimes the failure of a certain command does not indicate a problem. For example, you may use the `mkdir` command to ensure that a directory exists. If the directory already exists, `mkdir` will report an error, but you probably want `make` to continue regardless.

To ignore errors in a command line, write a '-' at the beginning of the line's text (after the initial tab). The '-' is discarded before the command is passed to the shell for execution.

For example,

```
clean:
        -rm -f *.o
```

This causes `rm` to continue even if it is unable to remove a file.

When you run `make` with the '-i' or '--ignore-errors' flag, errors are ignored in all commands of all rules. A rule in the makefile for the special target `.IGNORE` has the same effect, if there are no dependencies. These ways of ignoring errors are obsolete because '-' is more flexible.

When errors are to be ignored, because of either a '-' or the '-i' flag, `make` treats an error return just like success, except that it prints out a message that tells you the status code the command exited with, and says that the error has been ignored.

When an error happens that `make` has not been told to ignore, it implies that the current target cannot be correctly remade, and neither can any other that depends on it either directly or indirectly. No further commands will be executed for these targets, since their preconditions have not been achieved.

Normally `make` gives up immediately in this circumstance, returning a nonzero status. However, if the '-k' or '--keep-going' flag is specified, `make` continues to consider the other dependencies of the pending targets, remaking them if necessary, before it gives up and returns nonzero status. For example, after an error in compiling one object file, 'make -k' will continue compiling other object files even though it already knows that linking them will be impossible. See Section 9.7 [Summary of Options], page 89.

The usual behavior assumes that your purpose is to get the specified targets up to date; once `make` learns that this is impossible, it might as well report the failure immediately. The '-k' option says that the real purpose is to test as many of the changes made in the program as possible, perhaps to find several independent problems so that you can correct them all before the next attempt to compile. This is why Emacs' `compile` command passes the '-k' flag by default.

Usually when a command fails, if it has changed the target file at all, the file is corrupted and cannot be used—or at least it is not completely updated. Yet the file's timestamp says that it is now up to date, so the next time make runs, it will not try to update that file. The situation is just the same as when the command is killed by a signal; see Section 5.5 [Interrupts], page 42. So generally the right thing to do is to delete the target file if the command fails after beginning to change the file. make will do this if .DELETE_ON_ERROR appears as a target. This is almost always what you want make to do, but it is not historical practice; so for compatibility, you must explicitly request it.

5.5 Interrupting or Killing make

If make gets a fatal signal while a command is executing, it may delete the target file that the command was supposed to update. This is done if the target file's last-modification time has changed since make first checked it.

The purpose of deleting the target is to make sure that it is remade from scratch when make is next run. Why is this? Suppose you type *Ctrl-c* while a compiler is running, and it has begun to write an object file 'foo.o'. The *Ctrl-c* kills the compiler, resulting in an incomplete file whose last-modification time is newer than the source file 'foo.c'. But make also receives the *Ctrl-c* signal and deletes this incomplete file. If make did not do this, the next invocation of make would think that 'foo.o' did not require updating—resulting in a strange error message from the linker when it tries to link an object file half of which is missing.

You can prevent the deletion of a target file in this way by making the special target .PRECIOUS depend on it. Before remaking a target, make checks to see whether it appears on the dependencies of .PRECIOUS, and thereby decides whether the target should be deleted if a signal happens. Some reasons why you might do this are that the target is updated in some atomic fashion, or exists only to record a modification-time (its contents do not matter), or must exist at all times to prevent other sorts of trouble.

5.6 Recursive Use of make

Recursive use of make means using make as a command in a makefile. This technique is useful when you want separate makefiles for various subsystems that compose a larger system. For example, suppose you have a subdirectory 'subdir' which has its own makefile, and you would like the containing directory's makefile to run make on the subdirectory. You can do it by writing this:

```
subsystem:
        cd subdir && $(MAKE)
```

or, equivalently, this (see Section 9.7 [Summary of Options], page 89):

```
subsystem:
        $(MAKE) -C subdir
```

You can write recursive `make` commands just by copying this example, but there are many things to know about how they work and why, and about how the sub-`make` relates to the top-level `make`.

For your convenience, GNU `make` sets the variable `CURDIR` to the pathname of the current working directory for you. If `-C` is in effect, it will contain the path of the new directory, not the original. The value has the same precedence it would have if it were set in the makefile (by default, an environment variable `CURDIR` will not override this value). Note that setting this variable has no effect on the operation of `make`

5.6.1 How the `MAKE` Variable Works

Recursive `make` commands should always use the variable `MAKE`, not the explicit command name 'make', as shown here:

```
subsystem:
        cd subdir && $(MAKE)
```

The value of this variable is the file name with which `make` was invoked. If this file name was '/bin/make', then the command executed is 'cd subdir && /bin/make'. If you use a special version of `make` to run the top-level makefile, the same special version will be executed for recursive invocations.

As a special feature, using the variable `MAKE` in the commands of a rule alters the effects of the '-t' ('--touch'), '-n' ('--just-print'), or '-q' ('--question') option. Using the `MAKE` variable has the same effect as using a '+' character at the beginning of the command line. See Section 9.3 [Instead of Executing the Commands], page 85.

Consider the command 'make -t' in the above example. (The '-t' option marks targets as up to date without actually running any commands; see Section 9.3 [Instead of Execution], page 85.) Following the usual definition of '-t', a 'make -t' command in the example would create a file named 'subsystem' and do nothing else. What you really want it to do is run 'cd subdir && make -t'; but that would require executing the command, and '-t' says not to execute commands.

The special feature makes this do what you want: whenever a command line of a rule contains the variable `MAKE`, the flags '-t', '-n' and '-q' do not apply to that line. Command lines containing `MAKE` are executed normally despite the presence of a flag that causes most commands not to be run. The usual `MAKEFLAGS` mechanism passes the flags to the sub-`make` (see Section 5.6.3 [Communicating Options to a Sub-`make`], page 46), so your request to touch the files, or print the commands, is propagated to the subsystem.

5.6.2 Communicating Variables to a Sub-make

Variable values of the top-level make can be passed to the sub-make through the environment by explicit request. These variables are defined in the sub-make as defaults, but do not override what is specified in the makefile used by the sub-make makefile unless you use the '-e' switch (see Section 9.7 [Summary of Options], page 89).

To pass down, or *export*, a variable, make adds the variable and its value to the environment for running each command. The sub-make, in turn, uses the environment to initialize its table of variable values. See Section 6.9 [Variables from the Environment], page 62.

Except by explicit request, make exports a variable only if it is either defined in the environment initially or set on the command line, and if its name consists only of letters, numbers, and underscores. Some shells cannot cope with environment variable names consisting of characters other than letters, numbers, and underscores.

The special variables SHELL and MAKEFLAGS are always exported (unless you unexport them). MAKEFILES is exported if you set it to anything.

make automatically passes down variable values that were defined on the command line, by putting them in the MAKEFLAGS variable. See the next section.

Variables are *not* normally passed down if they were created by default by make (see Section 10.3 [Variables Used by Implicit Rules], page 100). The sub-make will define these for itself.

If you want to export specific variables to a sub-make, use the export directive, like this:

        export *variable* ...

If you want to *prevent* a variable from being exported, use the unexport directive, like this:

        unexport *variable* ...

As a convenience, you can define a variable and export it at the same time by doing:

        export *variable* = value

has the same result as:

        variable = value
        export *variable*

and

        export *variable* := value

has the same result as:

        variable := value
        export *variable*

Likewise,

```
export variable += value
```
is just like:
```
variable += value
export variable
```
See Section 6.6 [Appending More Text to Variables], page 59.

You may notice that the `export` and `unexport` directives work in `make` in the same way they work in the shell, `sh`.

If you want all variables to be exported by default, you can use `export` by itself:

```
export
```

This tells `make` that variables which are not explicitly mentioned in an `export` or `unexport` directive should be exported. Any variable given in an `unexport` directive will still *not* be exported. If you use `export` by itself to export variables by default, variables whose names contain characters other than alphanumerics and underscores will not be exported unless specifically mentioned in an `export` directive.

The behavior elicited by an `export` directive by itself was the default in older versions of GNU `make`. If your makefiles depend on this behavior and you want to be compatible with old versions of `make`, you can write a rule for the special target `.EXPORT_ALL_VARIABLES` instead of using the `export` directive. This will be ignored by old `makes`, while the `export` directive will cause a syntax error.

Likewise, you can use `unexport` by itself to tell `make` *not* to export variables by default. Since this is the default behavior, you would only need to do this if `export` had been used by itself earlier (in an included makefile, perhaps). You **cannot** use `export` and `unexport` by themselves to have variables exported for some commands and not for others. The last `export` or `unexport` directive that appears by itself determines the behavior for the entire run of `make`.

As a special feature, the variable `MAKELEVEL` is changed when it is passed down from level to level. This variable's value is a string which is the depth of the level as a decimal number. The value is '0' for the top-level `make`; '1' for a sub-make, '2' for a sub-sub-make, and so on. The incrementation happens when `make` sets up the environment for a command.

The main use of `MAKELEVEL` is to test it in a conditional directive (see Chapter 7 [Conditional Parts of Makefiles], page 65); this way you can write a makefile that behaves one way if run recursively and another way if run directly by you.

You can use the variable `MAKEFILES` to cause all sub-make commands to use additional makefiles. The value of `MAKEFILES` is a whitespace-separated list of file names. This variable, if defined in the outer-level makefile, is passed down through the environment; then it serves as a list of extra make-files for the sub-make to read before the usual or specified ones. See Section 3.4 [The Variable MAKEFILES], page 13.

5.6.3 Communicating Options to a Sub-make

Flags such as '-s' and '-k' are passed automatically to the sub-make through the variable MAKEFLAGS. This variable is set up automatically by make to contain the flag letters that make received. Thus, if you do 'make -ks' then MAKEFLAGS gets the value 'ks'.

As a consequence, every sub-make gets a value for MAKEFLAGS in its environment. In response, it takes the flags from that value and processes them as if they had been given as arguments. See Section 9.7 [Summary of Options], page 89.

Likewise variables defined on the command line are passed to the sub-make through MAKEFLAGS. Words in the value of MAKEFLAGS that contain '=', make treats as variable definitions just as if they appeared on the command line. See Section 9.5 [Overriding Variables], page 87.

The options '-C', '-f', '-o', and '-W' are not put into MAKEFLAGS; these options are not passed down.

The '-j' option is a special case (see Section 5.3 [Parallel Execution], page 39). If you set it to some numeric value, '-j 1' is always put into MAKEFLAGS instead of the value you specified. This is because if the '-j' option were passed down to sub-makes, you would get many more jobs running in parallel than you asked for. If you give '-j' with no numeric argument, meaning to run as many jobs as possible in parallel, this is passed down, since multiple infinities are no more than one.

If you do not want to pass the other flags down, you must change the value of MAKEFLAGS, like this:

```
subsystem:
        cd subdir && $(MAKE) MAKEFLAGS=
```

The command line variable definitions really appear in the variable MAKEOVERRIDES, and MAKEFLAGS contains a reference to this variable. If you do want to pass flags down normally, but don't want to pass down the command line variable definitions, you can reset MAKEOVERRIDES to empty, like this:

```
MAKEOVERRIDES =
```

This is not usually useful to do. However, some systems have a small fixed limit on the size of the environment, and putting so much information in into the value of MAKEFLAGS can exceed it. If you see the error message 'Arg list too long', this may be the problem. (For strict compliance with POSIX.2, changing MAKEOVERRIDES does not affect MAKEFLAGS if the special target '.POSIX' appears in the makefile. You probably do not care about this.)

A similar variable MFLAGS exists also, for historical compatibility. It has the same value as MAKEFLAGS except that it does not contain the command line variable definitions, and it always begins with a hyphen unless it is empty (MAKEFLAGS begins with a hyphen only when it begins with an option that has no single-letter version, such as '--warn-undefined-variables'). MFLAGS was traditionally used explicitly in the recursive make command, like this:

```
subsystem:
        cd subdir && $(MAKE) $(MFLAGS)
```

but now MAKEFLAGS makes this usage redundant. If you want your makefiles to be compatible with old make programs, use this technique; it will work fine with more modern make versions too.

The MAKEFLAGS variable can also be useful if you want to have certain options, such as '-k' (see Section 9.7 [Summary of Options], page 89), set each time you run make. You simply put a value for MAKEFLAGS in your environment. You can also set MAKEFLAGS in a makefile, to specify additional flags that should also be in effect for that makefile. (Note that you cannot use MFLAGS this way. That variable is set only for compatibility; make does not interpret a value you set for it in any way.)

When make interprets the value of MAKEFLAGS (either from the environment or from a makefile), it first prepends a hyphen if the value does not already begin with one. Then it chops the value into words separated by blanks, and parses these words as if they were options given on the command line (except that '-C', '-f', '-h', '-o', '-W', and their long-named versions are ignored; and there is no error for an invalid option).

If you do put MAKEFLAGS in your environment, you should be sure not to include any options that will drastically affect the actions of make and undermine the purpose of makefiles and of make itself. For instance, the '-t', '-n', and '-q' options, if put in one of these variables, could have disastrous consequences and would certainly have at least surprising and probably annoying effects.

5.6.4 The '--print-directory' Option

If you use several levels of recursive make invocations, the '-w' or '--print-directory' option can make the output a lot easier to understand by showing each directory as make starts processing it and as make finishes processing it. For example, if 'make -w' is run in the directory '/u/gnu/make', make will print a line of the form:

```
make: Entering directory '/u/gnu/make'.
```

before doing anything else, and a line of the form:

```
make: Leaving directory '/u/gnu/make'.
```
when processing is completed.

Normally, you do not need to specify this option because 'make' does it for you: '-w' is turned on automatically when you use the '-C' option, and in sub-makes. make will not automatically turn on '-w' if you also use '-s', which says to be silent, or if you use '--no-print-directory' to explicitly disable it.

5.7 Defining Canned Command Sequences

When the same sequence of commands is useful in making various targets, you can define it as a canned sequence with the define directive, and refer to the canned sequence from the rules for those targets. The canned sequence is actually a variable, so the name must not conflict with other variable names.

Here is an example of defining a canned sequence of commands:

```
define run-yacc
yacc $(firstword $^)
mv y.tab.c $@
endef
```

Here run-yacc is the name of the variable being defined; endef marks the end of the definition; the lines in between are the commands. The define directive does not expand variable references and function calls in the canned sequence; the '$' characters, parentheses, variable names, and so on, all become part of the value of the variable you are defining. See Section 6.8 [Defining Variables Verbatim], page 61, for a complete explanation of define.

The first command in this example runs Yacc on the first dependency of whichever rule uses the canned sequence. The output file from Yacc is always named 'y.tab.c'. The second command moves the output to the rule's target file name.

To use the canned sequence, substitute the variable into the commands of a rule. You can substitute it like any other variable (see Section 6.1 [Basics of Variable References], page 51). Because variables defined by define are recursively expanded variables, all the variable references you wrote inside the define are expanded now. For example:

```
foo.c : foo.y
        $(run-yacc)
```

'foo.y' will be substituted for the variable '$^' when it occurs in run-yacc's value, and 'foo.c' for '$@'.

This is a realistic example, but this particular one is not needed in practice because make has an implicit rule to figure out these commands based on the file names involved (see Chapter 10 [Using Implicit Rules], page 95).

In command execution, each line of a canned sequence is treated just as if the line appeared on its own in the rule, preceded by a tab. In particular, `make` invokes a separate subshell for each line. You can use the special prefix characters that affect command lines ('@', '-', and '+') on each line of a canned sequence. See Chapter 5 [Writing the Commands in Rules], page 37. For example, using this canned sequence:

```
define frobnicate
@echo "frobnicating target $@"
frob-step-1 $< -o $@-step-1
frob-step-2 $@-step-1 -o $@
endef
```

`make` will not echo the first line, the `echo` command. But it *will* echo the following two command lines.

On the other hand, prefix characters on the command line that refers to a canned sequence apply to every line in the sequence. So the rule:

```
frob.out: frob.in
@$(frobnicate)
```

does not echo *any* commands. (See Section 5.1 [Command Echoing], page 37, for a full explanation of '@'.)

5.8 Using Empty Commands

It is sometimes useful to define commands which do nothing. This is done simply by giving a command that consists of nothing but whitespace. For example:

```
target: ;
```

defines an empty command string for 'target'. You could also use a line beginning with a tab character to define an empty command string, but this would be confusing because such a line looks empty.

You may be wondering why you would want to define a command string that does nothing. The only reason this is useful is to prevent a target from getting implicit commands (from implicit rules or the .DEFAULT special target; see Chapter 10 [Implicit Rules], page 95 and see Section 10.6 [Defining Last-Resort Default Rules], page 110).

You may be inclined to define empty command strings for targets that are not actual files, but only exist so that their dependencies can be remade. However, this is not the best way to do that, because the dependencies may not be remade properly if the target file actually does exist. See Section 4.4 [Phony Targets], page 25, for a better way to do this.

6 How to Use Variables

A *variable* is a name defined in a makefile to represent a string of text, called the variable's *value*. These values are substituted by explicit request into targets, dependencies, commands, and other parts of the makefile. (In some other versions of **make**, variables are called *macros*.)

Variables and functions in all parts of a makefile are expanded when read, except for the shell commands in rules, the right-hand sides of variable definitions using '=', and the bodies of variable definitions using the **define** directive.

Variables can represent lists of file names, options to pass to compilers, programs to run, directories to look in for source files, directories to write output in, or anything else you can imagine.

A variable name may be any sequence of characters not containing ':', '#', '=', or leading or trailing whitespace. However, variable names containing characters other than letters, numbers, and underscores should be avoided, as they may be given special meanings in the future, and with some shells they cannot be passed through the environment to a sub-**make** (see Section 5.6.2 [Communicating Variables to a Sub-**make**], page 44).

Variable names are case-sensitive. The names 'foo', 'FOO', and 'Foo' all refer to different variables.

It is traditional to use upper case letters in variable names, but we recommend using lower case letters for variable names that serve internal purposes in the makefile, and reserving upper case for parameters that control implicit rules or for parameters that the user should override with command options (see Section 9.5 [Overriding Variables], page 87).

A few variables have names that are a single punctuation character or just a few characters. These are the *automatic variables*, and they have particular specialized uses. See Section 10.5.3 [Automatic Variables], page 106.

6.1 Basics of Variable References

To substitute a variable's value, write a dollar sign followed by the name of the variable in parentheses or braces: either '$(foo)' or '${foo}' is a valid reference to the variable foo. This special significance of '$' is why you must write '$$' to have the effect of a single dollar sign in a file name or command.

Variable references can be used in any context: targets, dependencies, commands, most directives, and new variable values. Here is an example of a common case, where a variable holds the names of all the object files in a program:

```
objects = program.o foo.o utils.o
program : $(objects)
        cc -o program $(objects)

$(objects) : defs.h
```

Variable references work by strict textual substitution. Thus, the rule

```
foo = c
prog.o : prog.$(foo)
        $(foo)$(foo) -$(foo) prog.$(foo)
```

could be used to compile a C program 'prog.c'. Since spaces before the variable value are ignored in variable assignments, the value of foo is precisely 'c'. (Don't actually write your makefiles this way!)

A dollar sign followed by a character other than a dollar sign, openparenthesis or open-brace treats that single character as the variable name. Thus, you could reference the variable x with '$x'. However, this practice is strongly discouraged, except in the case of the automatic variables (see Section 10.5.3 [Automatic Variables], page 106).

6.2 The Two Flavors of Variables

There are two ways that a variable in GNU make can have a value; we call them the two *flavors* of variables. The two flavors are distinguished in how they are defined and in what they do when expanded.

The first flavor of variable is a *recursively expanded* variable. Variables of this sort are defined by lines using '=' (see Section 6.5 [Setting Variables], page 58) or by the **define** directive (see Section 6.8 [Defining Variables Verbatim], page 61). The value you specify is installed verbatim; if it contains references to other variables, these references are expanded whenever this variable is substituted (in the course of expanding some other string). When this happens, it is called *recursive expansion*.

For example,

```
foo = $(bar)
bar = $(ugh)
ugh = Huh?

all:;echo $(foo)
```

will echo 'Huh?': '$(foo)' expands to '$(bar)' which expands to '$(ugh)' which finally expands to 'Huh?'.

This flavor of variable is the only sort supported by other versions of make. It has its advantages and its disadvantages. An advantage (most would say) is that:

```
CFLAGS = $(include_dirs) -O
```

```
include_dirs = -Ifoo -Ibar
```

will do what was intended: when 'CFLAGS' is expanded in a command, it will expand to '-Ifoo -Ibar -O'. A major disadvantage is that you cannot append something on the end of a variable, as in

```
CFLAGS = $(CFLAGS) -O
```

because it will cause an infinite loop in the variable expansion. (Actually make detects the infinite loop and reports an error.)

Another disadvantage is that any functions (see Chapter 8 [Functions for Transforming Text], page 71) referenced in the definition will be executed every time the variable is expanded. This makes make run slower; worse, it causes the wildcard and shell functions to give unpredictable results because you cannot easily control when they are called, or even how many times.

To avoid all the problems and inconveniences of recursively expanded variables, there is another flavor: simply expanded variables.

Simply expanded variables are defined by lines using ':=' (see Section 6.5 [Setting Variables], page 58). The value of a simply expanded variable is scanned once and for all, expanding any references to other variables and functions, when the variable is defined. The actual value of the simply expanded variable is the result of expanding the text that you write. It does not contain any references to other variables; it contains their values *as of the time this variable was defined*. Therefore,

```
x := foo
y := $(x) bar
x := later
```

is equivalent to

```
y := foo bar
x := later
```

When a simply expanded variable is referenced, its value is substituted verbatim.

Here is a somewhat more complicated example, illustrating the use of ':=' in conjunction with the shell function. (See Section 8.6 [The shell Function], page 81.) This example also shows use of the variable MAKELEVEL, which is changed when it is passed down from level to level. (See Section 5.6.2 [Communicating Variables to a Sub-make], page 44, for information about MAKELEVEL.)

```
ifeq (0,${MAKELEVEL})
cur-dir   := $(shell pwd)
whoami    := $(shell whoami)
host-type := $(shell arch)
MAKE := ${MAKE} host-type=${host-type} whoami=${whoami}
endif
```

An advantage of this use of ':=' is that a typical 'descend into a directory' command then looks like this:

```
${subdirs}:
        ${MAKE} cur-dir=${cur-dir}/$@ -C $@ all
```

Simply expanded variables generally make complicated makefile programming more predictable because they work like variables in most programming languages. They allow you to redefine a variable using its own value (or its value processed in some way by one of the expansion functions) and to use the expansion functions much more efficiently (see Chapter 8 [Functions for Transforming Text], page 71).

You can also use them to introduce controlled leading whitespace into variable values. Leading whitespace characters are discarded from your input before substitution of variable references and function calls; this means you can include leading spaces in a variable value by protecting them with variable references, like this:

```
nullstring :=
space := $(nullstring) # end of the line
```

Here the value of the variable space is precisely one space. The comment '# end of the line' is included here just for clarity. Since trailing space characters are *not* stripped from variable values, just a space at the end of the line would have the same effect (but be rather hard to read). If you put whitespace at the end of a variable value, it is a good idea to put a comment like that at the end of the line to make your intent clear. Conversely, if you do *not* want any whitespace characters at the end of your variable value, you must remember not to put a random comment on the end of the line after some whitespace, such as this:

```
dir := /foo/bar    # directory to put the frobs in
```

Here the value of the variable dir is '/foo/bar ' (with four trailing spaces), which was probably not the intention. (Imagine something like '$(dir)/file' with this definition!)

There is another assignment operator for variables, '?='. This is called a conditional variable assignment operator, because it only has an effect if the variable is not yet defined. This statement:

```
FOO ?= bar
```

is exactly equivalent to this (see Section 8.5 [The origin Function], page 79):

```
ifeq ($(origin FOO), undefined)
  FOO = bar
endif
```

Note that a variable set to an empty value is still defined, so '?=' will not set that variable.

6.3 Advanced Features for Reference to Variables

This section describes some advanced features you can use to reference variables in more flexible ways.

6.3.1 Substitution References

A *substitution reference* substitutes the value of a variable with alterations that you specify. It has the form '$(*var*:*a*=*b*)' (or '${*var*:*a*=*b*}') and its meaning is to take the value of the variable *var*, replace every *a* at the end of a word with *b* in that value, and substitute the resulting string.

When we say "at the end of a word", we mean that *a* must appear either followed by whitespace or at the end of the value in order to be replaced; other occurrences of *a* in the value are unaltered. For example:

```
foo := a.o b.o c.o
bar := $(foo:.o=.c)
```

sets 'bar' to 'a.c b.c c.c'. See Section 6.5 [Setting Variables], page 58.

A substitution reference is actually an abbreviation for use of the `patsubst` expansion function (see Section 8.2 [Functions for String Substitution and Analysis], page 72). We provide substitution references as well as `patsubst` for compatibility with other implementations of `make`.

Another type of substitution reference lets you use the full power of the `patsubst` function. It has the same form '$(*var*:*a*=*b*)' described above, except that now *a* must contain a single '%' character. This case is equivalent to '$(patsubst *a*,*b*,$(*var*))'. See Section 8.2 [Functions for String Substitution and Analysis], page 72, for a description of the `patsubst` function. For example:

```
foo := a.o b.o c.o
bar := $(foo:%.o=%.c)
```

sets 'bar' to 'a.c b.c c.c'.

6.3.2 Computed Variable Names

Computed variable names are a complicated concept needed only for sophisticated makefile programming. For most purposes you need not consider them, except to know that making a variable with a dollar sign in its name might have strange results. However, if you are the type that wants to understand everything, or you are actually interested in what they do, read on.

Variables may be referenced inside the name of a variable. This is called a *computed variable name* or a *nested variable reference*. For example,

```
x = y
```

```
y = z
a := $($(x))
```

defines a as 'z': the '$(x)' inside '$($(x))' expands to 'y', so '$($(x))'
expands to '$(y)' which in turn expands to 'z'. Here the name of the variable
to reference is not stated explicitly; it is computed by expansion of '$(x)'.
The reference '$(x)' here is nested within the outer variable reference.

The previous example shows two levels of nesting, but any number of
levels is possible. For example, here are three levels:

```
x = y
y = z
z = u
a := $($($(x)))
```

Here the innermost '$(x)' expands to 'y', so '$($(x))' expands to '$(y)'
which in turn expands to 'z'; now we have '$(z)', which becomes 'u'.

References to recursively-expanded variables within a variable name are
reexpanded in the usual fashion. For example:

```
x = $(y)
y = z
z = Hello
a := $($(x))
```

defines a as 'Hello': '$($(x))' becomes '$($(y))' which becomes '$(z)'
which becomes 'Hello'.

Nested variable references can also contain modified references and function invocations (see Chapter 8 [Functions for Transforming Text], page 71),
just like any other reference. For example, using the subst function (see
Section 8.2 [Functions for String Substitution and Analysis], page 72):

```
x = variable1
variable2 := Hello
y = $(subst 1,2,$(x))
z = y
a := $($($(z)))
```

eventually defines a as 'Hello'. It is doubtful that anyone would ever want to
write a nested reference as convoluted as this one, but it works: '$($($(z)))'
expands to '$($(y))' which becomes '$($(subst 1,2,$(x)))'. This gets the
value 'variable1' from x and changes it by substitution to 'variable2', so
that the entire string becomes '$(variable2)', a simple variable reference
whose value is 'Hello'.

A computed variable name need not consist entirely of a single variable
reference. It can contain several variable references, as well as some invariant
text. For example,

```
a_dirs := dira dirb
1_dirs := dir1 dir2
```

```
a_files := filea fileb
1_files := file1 file2

ifeq "$(use_a)" "yes"
a1 := a
else
a1 := 1
endif

ifeq "$(use_dirs)" "yes"
df := dirs
else
df := files
endif

dirs := $($(a1)_$(df))
```

will give `dirs` the same value as `a_dirs`, `1_dirs`, `a_files` or `1_files` depending on the settings of `use_a` and `use_dirs`.

Computed variable names can also be used in substitution references:

```
a_objects := a.o b.o c.o
1_objects := 1.o 2.o 3.o

sources := $($(a1)_objects:.o=.c)
```

defines `sources` as either 'a.c b.c c.c' or '1.c 2.c 3.c', depending on the value of `a1`.

The only restriction on this sort of use of nested variable references is that they cannot specify part of the name of a function to be called. This is because the test for a recognized function name is done before the expansion of nested references. For example,

```
ifdef do_sort
func := sort
else
func := strip
endif

bar := a d b g q c

foo := $($(func) $(bar))
```

attempts to give 'foo' the value of the variable 'sort a d b g q c' or 'strip a d b g q c', rather than giving 'a d b g q c' as the argument to either the sort or the strip function. This restriction could be removed in the future if that change is shown to be a good idea.

You can also use computed variable names in the left-hand side of a variable assignment, or in a `define` directive, as in:

```
dir = foo
$(dir)_sources := $(wildcard $(dir)/*.c)
define $(dir)_print
lpr $($(dir)_sources)
endef
```

This example defines the variables 'dir', 'foo_sources', and 'foo_print'.

Note that *nested variable references* are quite different from *recursively expanded variables* (see Section 6.2 [The Two Flavors of Variables], page 52), though both are used together in complex ways when doing makefile programming.

6.4 How Variables Get Their Values

Variables can get values in several different ways:

- You can specify an overriding value when you run `make`. See Section 9.5 [Overriding Variables], page 87.

- You can specify a value in the makefile, either with an assignment (see Section 6.5 [Setting Variables], page 58) or with a verbatim definition (see Section 6.8 [Defining Variables Verbatim], page 61).

- Variables in the environment become `make` variables. See Section 6.9 [Variables from the Environment], page 62.

- Several *automatic* variables are given new values for each rule. Each of these has a single conventional use. See Section 10.5.3 [Automatic Variables], page 106.

- Several variables have constant initial values. See Section 10.3 [Variables Used by Implicit Rules], page 100.

6.5 Setting Variables

To set a variable from the makefile, write a line starting with the variable name followed by '=' or ':='. Whatever follows the '=' or ':=' on the line becomes the value. For example,

```
objects = main.o foo.o bar.o utils.o
```

defines a variable named `objects`. Whitespace around the variable name and immediately after the '=' is ignored.

Variables defined with '=' are *recursively expanded* variables. Variables defined with ':=' are *simply expanded* variables; these definitions can contain variable references which will be expanded before the definition is made. See Section 6.2 [The Two Flavors of Variables], page 52.

The variable name may contain function and variable references, which are expanded when the line is read to find the actual variable name to use.

There is no limit on the length of the value of a variable except the amount of swapping space on the computer. When a variable definition is long, it is a good idea to break it into several lines by inserting backslash-newline at convenient places in the definition. This will not affect the functioning of `make`, but it will make the makefile easier to read.

Most variable names are considered to have the empty string as a value if you have never set them. Several variables have built-in initial values that are not empty, but you can set them in the usual ways (see Section 10.3 [Variables Used by Implicit Rules], page 100). Several special variables are set automatically to a new value for each rule; these are called the *automatic* variables (see Section 10.5.3 [Automatic Variables], page 106).

If you'd like a variable to be set to a value only if it's not already set, then you can use the shorthand operator '?=' instead of '='. These two settings of the variable 'FOO' are identical (see Section 8.5 [The `origin` Function], page 79):

```
FOO ?= bar
```

and

```
ifeq ($(origin FOO), undefined)
FOO = bar
endif
```

6.6 Appending More Text to Variables

Often it is useful to add more text to the value of a variable already defined. You do this with a line containing '+=', like this:

```
objects += another.o
```

This takes the value of the variable `objects`, and adds the text 'another.o' to it (preceded by a single space). Thus:

```
objects = main.o foo.o bar.o utils.o
objects += another.o
```

sets `objects` to 'main.o foo.o bar.o utils.o another.o'.

Using '+=' is similar to:

```
objects = main.o foo.o bar.o utils.o
objects := $(objects) another.o
```

but differs in ways that become important when you use more complex values.

When the variable in question has not been defined before, '+=' acts just like normal '=': it defines a recursively-expanded variable. However, when there *is* a previous definition, exactly what '+=' does depends on what flavor of variable you defined originally. See Section 6.2 [The Two Flavors of Variables], page 52, for an explanation of the two flavors of variables.

When you add to a variable's value with '+=', make acts essentially as if you had included the extra text in the initial definition of the variable. If you defined it first with ':=', making it a simply-expanded variable, '+=' adds to that simply-expanded definition, and expands the new text before appending it to the old value just as ':=' does (see Section 6.5 [Setting Variables], page 58, for a full explanation of ':='). In fact,

```
variable := value
variable += more
```

is exactly equivalent to:

```
variable := value
variable := $(variable) more
```

On the other hand, when you use '+=' with a variable that you defined first to be recursively-expanded using plain '=', make does something a bit different. Recall that when you define a recursively-expanded variable, make does not expand the value you set for variable and function references immediately. Instead it stores the text verbatim, and saves these variable and function references to be expanded later, when you refer to the new variable (see Section 6.2 [The Two Flavors of Variables], page 52). When you use '+=' on a recursively-expanded variable, it is this unexpanded text to which make appends the new text you specify.

```
variable = value
variable += more
```

is roughly equivalent to:

```
temp = value
variable = $(temp) more
```

except that of course it never defines a variable called temp. The importance of this comes when the variable's old value contains variable references. Take this common example:

```
CFLAGS = $(includes) -O
...
CFLAGS += -pg # enable profiling
```

The first line defines the CFLAGS variable with a reference to another variable, includes. (CFLAGS is used by the rules for C compilation; see Section 10.2 [Catalogue of Implicit Rules], page 96.) Using '=' for the definition makes CFLAGS a recursively-expanded variable, meaning '$(includes) -O' is *not* expanded when make processes the definition of CFLAGS. Thus, includes need not be defined yet for its value to take effect. It only has to be defined before any reference to CFLAGS. If we tried to append to the value of CFLAGS without using '+=', we might do it like this:

```
CFLAGS := $(CFLAGS) -pg # enable profiling
```

This is pretty close, but not quite what we want. Using ':=' redefines CFLAGS as a simply-expanded variable; this means make expands the text '$(CFLAGS) -pg' before setting the variable. If includes is not yet defined, we get ' -O -pg', and a later definition of includes will have no effect. Conversely, by using '+=' we set CFLAGS to the *unexpanded* value '$(includes) -O -pg'. Thus we preserve the reference to includes, so if that variable gets defined at any later point, a reference like '$(CFLAGS)' still uses its value.

6.7 The override Directive

If a variable has been set with a command argument (see Section 9.5 [Overriding Variables], page 87), then ordinary assignments in the makefile are ignored. If you want to set the variable in the makefile even though it was set with a command argument, you can use an **override** directive, which is a line that looks like this:

    override *variable* = *value*

or

    override *variable* := *value*

To append more text to a variable defined on the command line, use:

    override *variable* += *more text*

See Section 6.6 [Appending More Text to Variables], page 59.

The **override** directive was not invented for escalation in the war between makefiles and command arguments. It was invented so you can alter and add to values that the user specifies with command arguments.

For example, suppose you always want the '-g' switch when you run the C compiler, but you would like to allow the user to specify the other switches with a command argument just as usual. You could use this **override** directive:

    override CFLAGS += -g

You can also use **override** directives with **define** directives. This is done as you might expect:

    override define foo
    bar
    endef

See the next section for information about **define**.

6.8 Defining Variables Verbatim

Another way to set the value of a variable is to use the **define** directive. This directive has an unusual syntax which allows newline characters to be included in the value, which is convenient for defining canned sequences of commands (see Section 5.7 [Defining Canned Command Sequences], page 48).

The define directive is followed on the same line by the name of the variable and nothing more. The value to give the variable appears on the following lines. The end of the value is marked by a line containing just the word endef. Aside from this difference in syntax, define works just like '=': it creates a recursively-expanded variable (see Section 6.2 [The Two Flavors of Variables], page 52). The variable name may contain function and variable references, which are expanded when the directive is read to find the actual variable name to use.

```
define two-lines
echo foo
echo $(bar)
endef
```

The value in an ordinary assignment cannot contain a newline; but the newlines that separate the lines of the value in a define become part of the variable's value (except for the final newline which precedes the endef and is not considered part of the value).

The previous example is functionally equivalent to this:

```
two-lines = echo foo; echo $(bar)
```

since two commands separated by semicolon behave much like two separate shell commands. However, note that using two separate lines means make will invoke the shell twice, running an independent subshell for each line. See Section 5.2 [Command Execution], page 38.

If you want variable definitions made with define to take precedence over command-line variable definitions, you can use the override directive together with define:

```
override define two-lines
foo
$(bar)
endef
```

See Section 6.7 [The override Directive], page 61.

6.9 Variables from the Environment

Variables in make can come from the environment in which make is run. Every environment variable that make sees when it starts up is transformed into a make variable with the same name and value. But an explicit assignment in the makefile, or with a command argument, overrides the environment. (If the '-e' flag is specified, then values from the environment override assignments in the makefile. See Section 9.7 [Summary of Options], page 89. But this is not recommended practice.)

Thus, by setting the variable CFLAGS in your environment, you can cause all C compilations in most makefiles to use the compiler switches you prefer. This is safe for variables with standard or conventional meanings because you know that no makefile will use them for other things. (But this is not totally reliable; some makefiles set CFLAGS explicitly and therefore are not affected by the value in the environment.)

When make is invoked recursively, variables defined in the outer invocation can be passed to inner invocations through the environment (see Section 5.6 [Recursive Use of make], page 42). By default, only variables that came from the environment or the command line are passed to recursive invocations. You can use the export directive to pass other variables. See Section 5.6.2 [Communicating Variables to a Sub-make], page 44, for full details.

Other use of variables from the environment is not recommended. It is not wise for makefiles to depend for their functioning on environment variables set up outside their control, since this would cause different users to get different results from the same makefile. This is against the whole purpose of most makefiles.

Such problems would be especially likely with the variable SHELL, which is normally present in the environment to specify the user's choice of interactive shell. It would be very undesirable for this choice to affect make. So make ignores the environment value of SHELL (except on MS-DOS and MS-Windows, where SHELL is usually not set. See Section 5.2 [Special handling of SHELL on MS-DOS], page 38.)

6.10 Target-specific Variable Values

Variable values in make are usually global; that is, they are the same regardless of where they are evaluated (unless they're reset, of course). One exception to that is automatic variables (see Section 10.5.3 [Automatic Variables], page 106).

The other exception is *target-specific variable values*. This feature allows you to define different values for the same variable, based on the target that make is currently building. As with automatic variables, these values are only available within the context of a target's command script (and in other target-specific assignments).

Set a target-specific variable value like this:

    target ... : *variable-assignment*

or like this:

    target ... : override *variable-assignment*

Multiple *target* values create a target-specific variable value for each member of the target list individually.

The *variable-assignment* can be any valid form of assignment; recursive ('='), static (':='), appending ('+='), or conditional ('?='). All variables that appear within the *variable-assignment* are evaluated within the context of the target: thus, any previously-defined target-specific variable values will be in effect. Note that this variable is actually distinct from any "global" value: the two variables do not have to have the same flavor (recursive vs. static).

Target-specific variables have the same priority as any other makefile variable. Variables provided on the command-line (and in the environment if the '-e' option is in force) will take precedence. Specifying the `override` directive will allow the target-specific variable value to be preferred.

There is one more special feature of target-specific variables: when you define a target-specific variable, that variable value is also in effect for all dependencies of this target (unless those dependencies override it with their own target-specific variable value). So, for example, a statement like this:

```
prog : CFLAGS = -g
prog : prog.o foo.o bar.o
```

will set `CFLAGS` to '-g' in the command script for 'prog', but it will also set `CFLAGS` to '-g' in the command scripts that create 'prog.o', 'foo.o', and 'bar.o', and any command scripts which create their dependencies.

6.11 Pattern-specific Variable Values

In addition to target-specific variable values (see Section 6.10 [Target-specific Variable Values], page 63), GNU `make` supports pattern-specific variable values. In this form, a variable is defined for any target that matches the pattern specified. Variables defined in this way are searched after any target-specific variables defined explicitly for that target, and before target-specific variables defined for the parent target.

Set a pattern-specific variable value like this:

    pattern ... : *variable-assignment*

or like this:

    pattern ... : `override` *variable-assignment*

where *pattern* is a %-pattern. As with target-specific variable values, multiple *pattern* values create a pattern-specific variable value for each pattern individually. The *variable-assignment* can be any valid form of assignment. Any command-line variable setting will take precedence, unless `override` is specified.

For example:

```
%.o : CFLAGS = -O
```

will assign `CFLAGS` the value of '-O' for all targets matching the pattern %.o.

7 Conditional Parts of Makefiles

A *conditional* causes part of a makefile to be obeyed or ignored depending on the values of variables. Conditionals can compare the value of one variable to another, or the value of a variable to a constant string. Conditionals control what make actually "sees" in the makefile, so they *cannot* be used to control shell commands at the time of execution.

7.1 Example of a Conditional

The following example of a conditional tells make to use one set of libraries if the CC variable is 'gcc', and a different set of libraries otherwise. It works by controlling which of two command lines will be used as the command for a rule. The result is that 'CC=gcc' as an argument to make changes not only which compiler is used but also which libraries are linked.

```
libs_for_gcc = -lgnu
normal_libs =

foo: $(objects)
ifeq ($(CC),gcc)
        $(CC) -o foo $(objects) $(libs_for_gcc)
else
        $(CC) -o foo $(objects) $(normal_libs)
endif
```

This conditional uses three directives: one ifeq, one else and one endif.

The ifeq directive begins the conditional, and specifies the condition. It contains two arguments, separated by a comma and surrounded by parentheses. Variable substitution is performed on both arguments and then they are compared. The lines of the makefile following the ifeq are obeyed if the two arguments match; otherwise they are ignored.

The else directive causes the following lines to be obeyed if the previous conditional failed. In the example above, this means that the second alternative linking command is used whenever the first alternative is not used. It is optional to have an else in a conditional.

The endif directive ends the conditional. Every conditional must end with an endif. Unconditional makefile text follows.

As this example illustrates, conditionals work at the textual level: the lines of the conditional are treated as part of the makefile, or ignored, according to the condition. This is why the larger syntactic units of the makefile, such as rules, may cross the beginning or the end of the conditional.

When the variable CC has the value 'gcc', the above example has this effect:

```
foo: $(objects)
        $(CC) -o foo $(objects) $(libs_for_gcc)
```

When the variable CC has any other value, the effect is this:

```
foo: $(objects)
        $(CC) -o foo $(objects) $(normal_libs)
```

Equivalent results can be obtained in another way by conditionalizing a variable assignment and then using the variable unconditionally:

```
libs_for_gcc = -lgnu
normal_libs =

ifeq ($(CC),gcc)
  libs=$(libs_for_gcc)
else
  libs=$(normal_libs)
endif

foo: $(objects)
        $(CC) -o foo $(objects) $(libs)
```

7.2 Syntax of Conditionals

The syntax of a simple conditional with no else is as follows:

conditional-directive
text-if-true
endif

The *text-if-true* may be any lines of text, to be considered as part of the makefile if the condition is true. If the condition is false, no text is used instead.

The syntax of a complex conditional is as follows:

conditional-directive
text-if-true
else
text-if-false
endif

If the condition is true, *text-if-true* is used; otherwise, *text-if-false* is used instead. The *text-if-false* can be any number of lines of text.

The syntax of the *conditional-directive* is the same whether the conditional is simple or complex. There are four different directives that test different conditions. Here is a table of them:

```
ifeq (arg1, arg2)
ifeq 'arg1' 'arg2'
ifeq "arg1" "arg2"
ifeq "arg1" 'arg2'
ifeq 'arg1' "arg2"
```

Expand all variable references in *arg1* and *arg2* and compare them. If they are identical, the *text-if-true* is effective; otherwise, the *text-if-false*, if any, is effective.

Often you want to test if a variable has a non-empty value. When the value results from complex expansions of variables and functions, expansions you would consider empty may actually contain whitespace characters and thus are not seen as empty. However, you can use the `strip` function (see Section 8.2 [Text Functions], page 72) to avoid interpreting whitespace as a non-empty value. For example:

```
ifeq ($(strip $(foo)),)
text-if-empty
endif
```

will evaluate *text-if-empty* even if the expansion of `$(foo)` contains whitespace characters.

```
ifneq (arg1, arg2)
ifneq 'arg1' 'arg2'
ifneq "arg1" "arg2"
ifneq "arg1" 'arg2'
ifneq 'arg1' "arg2"
```

Expand all variable references in *arg1* and *arg2* and compare them. If they are different, the *text-if-true* is effective; otherwise, the *text-if-false*, if any, is effective.

`ifdef` *variable-name*

If the variable *variable-name* has a non-empty value, the *text-if-true* is effective; otherwise, the *text-if-false*, if any, is effective. Variables that have never been defined have an empty value.

Note that `ifdef` only tests whether a variable has a value. It does not expand the variable to see if that value is nonempty. Consequently, tests using `ifdef` return true for all definitions except those like `foo =`. To test for an empty value, use `ifeq ($(foo),)`. For example,

```
bar =
foo = $(bar)
ifdef foo
frobozz = yes
else
```

```
        frobozz = no
        endif
```

sets 'frobozz' to 'yes', while:

```
        foo =
        ifdef foo
        frobozz = yes
        else
        frobozz = no
        endif
```

sets 'frobozz' to 'no'.

ifndef *variable-name*

If the variable *variable-name* has an empty value, the *text-if-true* is effective; otherwise, the *text-if-false*, if any, is effective.

Extra spaces are allowed and ignored at the beginning of the conditional directive line, but a tab is not allowed. (If the line begins with a tab, it will be considered a command for a rule.) Aside from this, extra spaces or tabs may be inserted with no effect anywhere except within the directive name or within an argument. A comment starting with '#' may appear at the end of the line.

The other two directives that play a part in a conditional are else and endif. Each of these directives is written as one word, with no arguments. Extra spaces are allowed and ignored at the beginning of the line, and spaces or tabs at the end. A comment starting with '#' may appear at the end of the line.

Conditionals affect which lines of the makefile make uses. If the condition is true, make reads the lines of the *text-if-true* as part of the makefile; if the condition is false, make ignores those lines completely. It follows that syntactic units of the makefile, such as rules, may safely be split across the beginning or the end of the conditional.

make evaluates conditionals when it reads a makefile. Consequently, you cannot use automatic variables in the tests of conditionals because they are not defined until commands are run (see Section 10.5.3 [Automatic Variables], page 106).

To prevent intolerable confusion, it is not permitted to start a conditional in one makefile and end it in another. However, you may write an include directive within a conditional, provided you do not attempt to terminate the conditional inside the included file.

7.3 Conditionals that Test Flags

You can write a conditional that tests make command flags such as '-t' by using the variable MAKEFLAGS together with the findstring function (see

Section 8.2 [Functions for String Substitution and Analysis], page 72). This is useful when `touch` is not enough to make a file appear up to date.

The `findstring` function determines whether one string appears as a substring of another. If you want to test for the '-t' flag, use 't' as the first string and the value of `MAKEFLAGS` as the other.

For example, here is how to arrange to use 'ranlib -t' to finish marking an archive file up to date:

```
archive.a: ...
ifneq (,$(findstring t,$(MAKEFLAGS)))
        +touch archive.a
        +ranlib -t archive.a
else
        ranlib archive.a
endif
```

The '+' prefix marks those command lines as "recursive" so that they will be executed despite use of the '-t' flag. See Section 5.6 [Recursive Use of make], page 42.

8 Functions for Transforming Text

Functions allow you to do text processing in the makefile to compute the files to operate on or the commands to use. You use a function in a *function call*, where you give the name of the function and some text (the *arguments*) for the function to operate on. The result of the function's processing is substituted into the makefile at the point of the call, just as a variable might be substituted.

8.1 Function Call Syntax

A function call resembles a variable reference. It looks like this:

$(*function arguments*)

or like this:

${*function arguments*}

Here *function* is a function name; one of a short list of names that are part of make. There is no provision for defining new functions.

The *arguments* are the arguments of the function. They are separated from the function name by one or more spaces or tabs, and if there is more than one argument, then they are separated by commas. Such whitespace and commas are not part of an argument's value. The delimiters which you use to surround the function call, whether parentheses or braces, can appear in an argument only in matching pairs; the other kind of delimiters may appear singly. If the arguments themselves contain other function calls or variable references, it is wisest to use the same kind of delimiters for all the references; write '$(subst a,b,$(x))', not '$(subst a,b,${x})'. This is because it is clearer, and because only one type of delimiter is matched to find the end of the reference.

The text written for each argument is processed by substitution of variables and function calls to produce the argument value, which is the text on which the function acts. The substitution is done in the order in which the arguments appear.

Commas and unmatched parentheses or braces cannot appear in the text of an argument as written; leading spaces cannot appear in the text of the first argument as written. These characters can be put into the argument value by variable substitution. First define variables comma and space whose values are isolated comma and space characters, then substitute these variables where such characters are wanted, like this:

```
comma:= ,
empty:=
space:= $(empty) $(empty)
foo:= a b c
bar:= $(subst $(space),$(comma),$(foo))
# bar is now 'a,b,c'.
```

Here the `subst` function replaces each space with a comma, through the value of `foo`, and substitutes the result.

8.2 Functions for String Substitution and Analysis

Here are some functions that operate on strings:

$(subst *from*, *to*, *text*)

>   Performs a textual replacement on the text *text*: each occur-
>   rence of *from* is replaced by *to*. The result is substituted for the
>   function call. For example,
>
> $(subst ee,EE,feet on the street)
>
>   substitutes the string 'fEEt on the strEEt'.

$(patsubst *pattern*, *replacement*, *text*)

>   Finds whitespace-separated words in *text* that match *pattern*
>   and replaces them with *replacement*. Here *pattern* may contain
>   a '%' which acts as a wildcard, matching any number of any
>   characters within a word. If *replacement* also contains a '%', the
>   '%' is replaced by the text that matched the '%' in *pattern*.
>
>   '%' characters in `patsubst` function invocations can be quoted
>   with preceding backslashes ('\'). Backslashes that would other-
>   wise quote '%' characters can be quoted with more backslashes.
>   Backslashes that quote '%' characters or other backslashes are
>   removed from the pattern before it is compared file names or
>   has a stem substituted into it. Backslashes that are not in dan-
>   ger of quoting '%' characters go unmolested. For example, the
>   pattern 'the\%weird\\%pattern\\' has 'the%weird\' preceding
>   the operative '%' character, and 'pattern\\' following it. The
>   final two backslashes are left alone because they cannot affect
>   any '%' character.
>
>   Whitespace between words is folded into single space characters;
>   leading and trailing whitespace is discarded.
>
>   For example,
>
> $(patsubst %.c,%.o,x.c.c bar.c)
>
>   produces the value 'x.c.o bar.o'.

Substitution references (see Section 6.3.1 [Substitution References], page 55) are a simpler way to get the effect of the `patsubst` function:

$(*var*:*pattern*=*replacement*)

is equivalent to

$(patsubst *pattern*,*replacement*,$(*var*))

The second shorthand simplifies one of the most common uses of `patsubst`: replacing the suffix at the end of file names.

$(*var*:*suffix*=*replacement*)

is equivalent to

$(patsubst %*suffix*,%*replacement*,$(*var*))

For example, you might have a list of object files:

```
objects = foo.o bar.o baz.o
```

To get the list of corresponding source files, you could simply write:

```
$(objects:.o=.c)
```

instead of using the general form:

```
$(patsubst %.o,%.c,$(objects))
```

$(strip *string*)

> Removes leading and trailing whitespace from *string* and replaces each internal sequence of one or more whitespace characters with a single space. Thus, '$(strip a b c)' results in 'a b c'.
>
> The function `strip` can be very useful when used in conjunction with conditionals. When comparing something with the empty string '' using `ifeq` or `ifneq`, you usually want a string of just whitespace to match the empty string (see Chapter 7 [Conditionals], page 65).
>
> Thus, the following may fail to have the desired results:
>
> ```
> .PHONY: all
> ifneq   "$(needs_made)" ""
> all: $(needs_made)
> else
> all:;@echo 'Nothing to make!'
> endif
> ```
>
> Replacing the variable reference '$(needs_made)' with the function call '$(strip $(needs_made))' in the `ifneq` directive would make it more robust.

$(findstring *find*,*in*)

> Searches *in* for an occurrence of *find*. If it occurs, the value is
> *find*; otherwise, the value is empty. You can use this function in
> a conditional to test for the presence of a specific substring in a
> given string. Thus, the two examples,
>
> ```
> $(findstring a,a b c)
> $(findstring a,b c)
> ```
>
> produce the values 'a' and '' (the empty string), respectively. See
> Section 7.3 [Testing Flags], page 68, for a practical application
> of findstring.

$(filter *pattern*..., *text*)

> Removes all whitespace-separated words in *text* that do *not*
> match any of the *pattern* words, returning only matching words.
> The patterns are written using '%', just like the patterns used in
> the patsubst function above.
>
> The filter function can be used to separate out different types
> of strings (such as file names) in a variable. For example:
>
> ```
> sources := foo.c bar.c baz.s ugh.h
> foo: $(sources)
>         cc $(filter %.c %.s,$(sources)) -o foo
> ```
>
> says that 'foo' depends of 'foo.c', 'bar.c', 'baz.s' and 'ugh.h'
> but only 'foo.c', 'bar.c' and 'baz.s' should be specified in the
> command to the compiler.

$(filter-out *pattern*..., *text*)

> Removes all whitespace-separated words in *text* that *do* match
> the *pattern* words, returning only the words that *do not* match.
> This is the exact opposite of the filter function.
>
> For example, given:
>
> ```
> objects=main1.o foo.o main2.o bar.o
> mains=main1.o main2.o
> ```
>
> the following generates a list which contains all the object files
> not in 'mains':
>
> ```
> $(filter-out $(mains),$(objects))
> ```

$(sort *list*)

> Sorts the words of *list* in lexical order, removing duplicate words.
> The output is a list of words separated by single spaces. Thus,
>
> ```
> $(sort foo bar lose)
> ```
>
> returns the value 'bar foo lose'.
>
> Incidentally, since sort removes duplicate words, you can use it
> for this purpose even if you don't care about the sort order.

Here is a realistic example of the use of **subst** and **patsubst**. Suppose that a makefile uses the **VPATH** variable to specify a list of directories that **make** should search for dependency files (see Section 4.3.1 [VPATH Search Path for All Dependencies], page 21). This example shows how to tell the C compiler to search for header files in the same list of directories.

The value of **VPATH** is a list of directories separated by colons, such as 'src:../headers'. First, the **subst** function is used to change the colons to spaces:

```
$(subst :, ,$(VPATH))
```

This produces 'src ../headers'. Then **patsubst** is used to turn each directory name into a '-I' flag. These can be added to the value of the variable **CFLAGS**, which is passed automatically to the C compiler, like this:

```
override CFLAGS += $(patsubst %,-I%,$(subst :, ,$(VPATH)))
```

The effect is to append the text '-Isrc -I../headers' to the previously given value of **CFLAGS**. The **override** directive is used so that the new value is assigned even if the previous value of **CFLAGS** was specified with a command argument (see Section 6.7 [The **override** Directive], page 61).

8.3 Functions for File Names

Several of the built-in expansion functions relate specifically to taking apart file names or lists of file names.

Each of the following functions performs a specific transformation on a file name. The argument of the function is regarded as a series of file names, separated by whitespace. (Leading and trailing whitespace is ignored.) Each file name in the series is transformed in the same way and the results are concatenated with single spaces between them.

$(dir names...)

> Extracts the directory-part of each file name in *names*. The directory-part of the file name is everything up through (and including) the last slash in it. If the file name contains no slash, the directory part is the string './'. For example,
>
> > $(dir src/foo.c hacks)
>
> produces the result 'src/ ./'.

$(notdir names...)

> Extracts all but the directory-part of each file name in *names*. If the file name contains no slash, it is left unchanged. Otherwise, everything through the last slash is removed from it.
>
> A file name that ends with a slash becomes an empty string. This is unfortunate, because it means that the result does not always have the same number of whitespace-separated file names

as the argument had; but we do not see any other valid alternative.

For example,

```
$(notdir src/foo.c hacks)
```

produces the result 'foo.c hacks'.

$(suffix *names*...)

> Extracts the suffix of each file name in *names*. If the file name contains a period, the suffix is everything starting with the last period. Otherwise, the suffix is the empty string. This frequently means that the result will be empty when *names* is not, and if *names* contains multiple file names, the result may contain fewer file names.
>
> For example,

```
$(suffix src/foo.c src-1.0/bar.c hacks)
```

produces the result '.c .c'.

$(basename *names*...)

> Extracts all but the suffix of each file name in *names*. If the file name contains a period, the basename is everything starting up to (and not including) the last period. Periods in the directory part are ignored. If there is no period, the basename is the entire file name. For example,

```
$(basename src/foo.c src-1.0/bar hacks)
```

produces the result 'src/foo src-1.0/bar hacks'.

$(addsuffix *suffix*,*names*...)

> The argument *names* is regarded as a series of names, separated by whitespace; *suffix* is used as a unit. The value of *suffix* is appended to the end of each individual name and the resulting larger names are concatenated with single spaces between them. For example,

```
$(addsuffix .c,foo bar)
```

produces the result 'foo.c bar.c'.

$(addprefix *prefix*,*names*...)

> The argument *names* is regarded as a series of names, separated by whitespace; *prefix* is used as a unit. The value of *prefix* is prepended to the front of each individual name and the resulting larger names are concatenated with single spaces between them. For example,

```
$(addprefix src/,foo bar)
```

produces the result 'src/foo src/bar'.

$(join *list1*, *list2*)

> Concatenates the two arguments word by word: the two first
> words (one from each argument) concatenated form the first
> word of the result, the two second words form the second word
> of the result, and so on. So the *n*th word of the result comes
> from the *n*th word of each argument. If one argument has more
> words that the other, the extra words are copied unchanged into
> the result.
>
> For example, '$(join a b,.c .o)' produces 'a.c b.o'.
>
> Whitespace between the words in the lists is not preserved; it is
> replaced with a single space.
>
> This function can merge the results of the dir and notdir func-
> tions, to produce the original list of files which was given to
> those two functions.

$(word *n*, *text*)

> Returns the *n*th word of *text*. The legitimate values of *n* start
> from 1. If *n* is bigger than the number of words in *text*, the
> value is empty. For example,
>
> ```
> $(word 2, foo bar baz)
> ```
>
> returns 'bar'.

$(wordlist *s*,*e*, *text*)

> Returns the list of words in *text* starting with word *s* and ending
> with word *e* (inclusive). The legitimate values of *s* and *e* start
> from 1. If *s* is bigger than the number of words in *text*, the value
> is empty. If *e* is bigger than the number of words in *text*, words
> up to the end of *text* are returned. If *s* is greater than *e*, make
> swaps them for you. For example,
>
> ```
> $(wordlist 2, 3, foo bar baz)
> ```
>
> returns 'bar baz'.

$(words *text*)

> Returns the number of words in *text*. Thus, the last word of
> *text* is $(word $(words *text*), *text*).

$(firstword *names*...)

> The argument *names* is regarded as a series of names, separated
> by whitespace. The value is the first name in the series. The
> rest of the names are ignored.
>
> For example,
>
> ```
> $(firstword foo bar)
> ```
>
> produces the result 'foo'. Although $(firstword *text*) is the
> same as $(word 1, *text*), the firstword function is retained for
> its simplicity.

$(wildcard *pattern*)

> The argument *pattern* is a file name pattern, typically containing wildcard characters (as in shell file name patterns). The result of `wildcard` is a space-separated list of the names of existing files that match the pattern. See Section 4.2 [Using Wildcard Characters in File Names], page 18.

8.4 The `foreach` Function

The `foreach` function is very different from other functions. It causes one piece of text to be used repeatedly, each time with a different substitution performed on it. It resembles the `for` command in the shell `sh` and the `foreach` command in the C-shell `csh`.

The syntax of the `foreach` function is:

    $(foreach *var*,*list*,*text*)

The first two arguments, *var* and *list*, are expanded before anything else is done; note that the last argument, *text*, is **not** expanded at the same time. Then for each word of the expanded value of *list*, the variable named by the expanded value of *var* is set to that word, and *text* is expanded. Presumably *text* contains references to that variable, so its expansion will be different each time.

The result is that *text* is expanded as many times as there are whitespace-separated words in *list*. The multiple expansions of *text* are concatenated, with spaces between them, to make the result of `foreach`.

This simple example sets the variable 'files' to the list of all files in the directories in the list 'dirs':

    dirs := a b c d
    files := $(foreach dir,$(dirs),$(wildcard $(dir)/*))

Here *text* is '$(wildcard $(dir)/*)'. The first repetition finds the value 'a' for dir, so it produces the same result as '$(wildcard a/*)'; the second repetition produces the result of '$(wildcard b/*)'; and the third, that of '$(wildcard c/*)'.

This example has the same result (except for setting 'dirs') as the following example:

    files := $(wildcard a/* b/* c/* d/*)

When *text* is complicated, you can improve readability by giving it a name, with an additional variable:

    find_files = $(wildcard $(dir)/*)
    dirs := a b c d
    files := $(foreach dir,$(dirs),$(find_files))

Here we use the variable `find_files` this way. We use plain '=' to define a recursively-expanding variable, so that its value contains an actual function call to be reexpanded under the control of `foreach`; a simply-expanded variable would not do, since `wildcard` would be called only once at the time of defining `find_files`.

The `foreach` function has no permanent effect on the variable *var*; its value and flavor after the `foreach` function call are the same as they were beforehand. The other values which are taken from *list* are in effect only temporarily, during the execution of `foreach`. The variable *var* is a simply-expanded variable during the execution of `foreach`. If *var* was undefined before the `foreach` function call, it is undefined after the call. See Section 6.2 [The Two Flavors of Variables], page 52.

You must take care when using complex variable expressions that result in variable names because many strange things are valid variable names, but are probably not what you intended. For example,

```
files := $(foreach Esta escrito en espanol!,b c ch,$(find_files))
```

might be useful if the value of `find_files` references the variable whose name is 'Esta escrito en espanol!' (es un nombre bastante largo, no?), but it is more likely to be a mistake.

8.5 The `origin` Function

The `origin` function is unlike most other functions in that it does not operate on the values of variables; it tells you something *about* a variable. Specifically, it tells you where it came from.

The syntax of the `origin` function is:

`$(origin` *variable*`)`

Note that *variable* is the *name* of a variable to inquire about; not a *reference* to that variable. Therefore you would not normally use a '`$`' or parentheses when writing it. (You can, however, use a variable reference in the name if you want the name not to be a constant.)

The result of this function is a string telling you how the variable *variable* was defined:

'`undefined`'

> if *variable* was never defined.

'`default`'

> if *variable* has a default definition, as is usual with `CC` and so on. See Section 10.3 [Variables Used by Implicit Rules], page 100. Note that if you have redefined a default variable, the `origin` function will return the origin of the later definition.

'`environment`'

> if *variable* was defined as an environment variable and the '`-e`' option is *not* turned on (see Section 9.7 [Summary of Options], page 89).

'environment override'

>if *variable* was defined as an environment variable and the '-e'
>option *is* turned on (see Section 9.7 [Summary of Options],
>page 89).

'file'

>if *variable* was defined in a makefile.

'command line'

>if *variable* was defined on the command line.

'override'

>if *variable* was defined with an override directive in a makefile
>(see Section 6.7 [The override Directive], page 61).

'automatic'

>if *variable* is an automatic variable defined for the execution
>of the commands for each rule (see Section 10.5.3 [Automatic
>Variables], page 106).

This information is primarily useful (other than for your curiosity) to determine if you want to believe the value of a variable. For example, suppose you have a makefile 'foo' that includes another makefile 'bar'. You want a variable bletch to be defined in 'bar' if you run the command 'make -f bar', even if the environment contains a definition of bletch. However, if 'foo' defined bletch before including 'bar', you do not want to override that definition. This could be done by using an override directive in 'foo', giving that definition precedence over the later definition in 'bar'; unfortunately, the override directive would also override any command line definitions. So, 'bar' could include:

```
ifdef bletch
ifeq "$(origin bletch)" "environment"
bletch = barf, gag, etc.
endif
endif
```

If bletch has been defined from the environment, this will redefine it.

If you want to override a previous definition of bletch if it came from the environment, even under '-e', you could instead write:

```
ifneq "$(findstring environment,$(origin bletch))" ""
bletch = barf, gag, etc.
endif
```

Here the redefinition takes place if '$(origin bletch)' returns either 'environment' or 'environment override'. See Section 8.2 [Functions for String Substitution and Analysis], page 72.

8.6 The `shell` Function

The `shell` function is unlike any other function except the `wildcard` function (see Section 4.2.3 [The Function `wildcard`], page 20) in that it communicates with the world outside of `make`.

The `shell` function performs the same function that backquotes ('`') perform in most shells: it does *command expansion*. This means that it takes an argument that is a shell command and returns the output of the command. The only processing `make` does on the result, before substituting it into the surrounding text, is to convert each newline or carriage-return / newline pair to a single space. It also removes the trailing (carriage-return and) newline, if it's the last thing in the result.

The commands run by calls to the `shell` function are run when the function calls are expanded. In most cases, this is when the makefile is read in. The exception is that function calls in the commands of the rules are expanded when the commands are run, and this applies to `shell` function calls like all others.

Here are some examples of the use of the `shell` function:

```
contents := $(shell cat foo)
```

sets `contents` to the contents of the file 'foo', with a space (rather than a newline) separating each line.

```
files := $(shell echo *.c)
```

sets `files` to the expansion of '*.c'. Unless `make` is using a very strange shell, this has the same result as '`$(wildcard *.c)`'.

9 How to Run make

A makefile that says how to recompile a program can be used in more than one way. The simplest use is to recompile every file that is out of date. Usually, makefiles are written so that if you run make with no arguments, it does just that.

But you might want to update only some of the files; you might want to use a different compiler or different compiler options; you might want just to find out which files are out of date without changing them.

By giving arguments when you run make, you can do any of these things and many others.

The exit status of make is always one of three values:

0   The exit status is zero if make is successful.

2   The exit status is two if make encounters any errors. It will print messages describing the particular errors.

1   The exit status is one if you use the '-q' flag and make determines that some target is not already up to date. See Section 9.3 [Instead of Executing the Commands], page 85.

9.1 Arguments to Specify the Makefile

The way to specify the name of the makefile is with the '-f' or '--file' option ('--makefile' also works). For example, '-f altmake' says to use the file 'altmake' as the makefile.

If you use the '-f' flag several times and follow each '-f' with an argument, all the specified files are used jointly as makefiles.

If you do not use the '-f' or '--file' flag, the default is to try 'GNUmakefile', 'makefile', and 'Makefile', in that order, and use the first of these three which exists or can be made (see Chapter 3 [Writing Makefiles], page 11).

9.2 Arguments to Specify the Goals

The *goals* are the targets that make should strive ultimately to update. Other targets are updated as well if they appear as dependencies of goals, or dependencies of dependencies of goals, etc.

By default, the goal is the first target in the makefile (not counting targets that start with a period). Therefore, makefiles are usually written so that the first target is for compiling the entire program or programs they describe. If the first rule in the makefile has several targets, only the first target in the rule becomes the default goal, not the whole list.

You can specify a different goal or goals with arguments to make. Use the name of the goal as an argument. If you specify several goals, make processes each of them in turn, in the order you name them.

Any target in the makefile may be specified as a goal (unless it starts with '-' or contains an '=', in which case it will be parsed as a switch or variable definition, respectively). Even targets not in the makefile may be specified, if make can find implicit rules that say how to make them.

Make will set the special variable MAKECMDGOALS to the list of goals you specified on the command line. If no goals were given on the command line, this variable is empty. Note that this variable should be used only in special circumstances.

An example of appropriate use is to avoid including '.d' files during clean rules (see Section 4.12 [Automatic Dependencies], page 34), so make won't create them only to immediately remove them again:

```
sources = foo.c bar.c


ifneq ($(MAKECMDGOALS),clean)
include $(sources:.c=.d)
endif
```

One use of specifying a goal is if you want to compile only a part of the program, or only one of several programs. Specify as a goal each file that you wish to remake. For example, consider a directory containing several programs, with a makefile that starts like this:

```
.PHONY: all
all: size nm ld ar as
```

If you are working on the program size, you might want to say 'make size' so that only the files of that program are recompiled.

Another use of specifying a goal is to make files that are not normally made. For example, there may be a file of debugging output, or a version of the program that is compiled specially for testing, which has a rule in the makefile but is not a dependency of the default goal.

Another use of specifying a goal is to run the commands associated with a phony target (see Section 4.4 [Phony Targets], page 25) or empty target (see Section 4.6 [Empty Target Files to Record Events], page 27). Many makefiles contain a phony target named 'clean' which deletes everything except source files. Naturally, this is done only if you request it explicitly with 'make clean'. Following is a list of typical phony and empty target names. See Section 14.5 [Standard Targets], page 132, for a detailed list of all the standard target names which GNU software packages use.

'all'   Make all the top-level targets the makefile knows about.

'clean'   Delete all files that are normally created by running make.

'mostlyclean'
> Like 'clean', but may refrain from deleting a few files that
> people normally don't want to recompile. For example, the
> 'mostlyclean' target for GCC does not delete 'libgcc.a', be-
> cause recompiling it is rarely necessary and takes a lot of time.

'distclean'
'realclean'
'clobber'   Any of these targets might be defined to delete *more* files than
> 'clean' does. For example, this would delete configuration files
> or links that you would normally create as preparation for com-
> pilation, even if the makefile itself cannot create these files.

'install'   Copy the executable file into a directory that users typically
> search for commands; copy any auxiliary files that the executable
> uses into the directories where it will look for them.

'print'   Print listings of the source files that have changed.

'tar'   Create a tar file of the source files.

'shar'   Create a shell archive (shar file) of the source files.

'dist'   Create a distribution file of the source files. This might be a tar
> file, or a shar file, or a compressed version of one of the above,
> or even more than one of the above.

'TAGS'   Update a tags table for this program.

'check'
'test'   Perform self tests on the program this makefile builds.

9.3 Instead of Executing the Commands

The makefile tells make how to tell whether a target is up to date, and
how to update each target. But updating the targets is not always what you
want. Certain options specify other activities for make.

'-n'
'--just-print'
'--dry-run'
'--recon'
> "No-op". The activity is to print what commands would be used
> to make the targets up to date, but not actually execute them.

'-t'
'--touch'

> "Touch". The activity is to mark the targets as up to date
> without actually changing them. In other words, make pretends
> to compile the targets but does not really change their contents.

'`-q`'
'`--question`'

"Question". The activity is to find out silently whether the targets are up to date already; but execute no commands in either case. In other words, neither compilation nor output will occur.

'`-W` *file*'
'`--what-if=`*file*'
'`--assume-new=`*file*'
'`--new-file=`*file*'

"What if". Each '`-W`' flag is followed by a file name. The given files' modification times are recorded by make as being the present time, although the actual modification times remain the same. You can use the '`-W`' flag in conjunction with the '`-n`' flag to see what would happen if you were to modify specific files.

With the '`-n`' flag, make prints the commands that it would normally execute but does not execute them.

With the '`-t`' flag, make ignores the commands in the rules and uses (in effect) the command `touch` for each target that needs to be remade. The `touch` command is also printed, unless '`-s`' or `.SILENT` is used. For speed, make does not actually invoke the program `touch`. It does the work directly.

With the '`-q`' flag, make prints nothing and executes no commands, but the exit status code it returns is zero if and only if the targets to be considered are already up to date. If the exit status is one, then some updating needs to be done. If make encounters an error, the exit status is two, so you can distinguish an error from a target that is not up to date.

It is an error to use more than one of these three flags in the same invocation of make.

The '`-n`', '`-t`', and '`-q`' options do not affect command lines that begin with '`+`' characters or contain the strings '`$(MAKE)`' or '`${MAKE}`'. Note that only the line containing the '`+`' character or the strings '`$(MAKE)`' or '`${MAKE}`' is run regardless of these options. Other lines in the same rule are not run unless they too begin with '`+`' or contain '`$(MAKE)`' or '`${MAKE}`' (See Section 5.6.1 [How the MAKE Variable Works], page 43.)

The '`-W`' flag provides two features:

- If you also use the '`-n`' or '`-q`' flag, you can see what make would do if you were to modify some files.

- Without the '`-n`' or '`-q`' flag, when make is actually executing commands, the '`-W`' flag can direct make to act as if some files had been modified, without actually modifying the files.

Note that the options '-p' and '-v' allow you to obtain other information about make or about the makefiles in use (see Section 9.7 [Summary of Options], page 89).

9.4 Avoiding Recompilation of Some Files

Sometimes you may have changed a source file but you do not want to recompile all the files that depend on it. For example, suppose you add a macro or a declaration to a header file that many other files depend on. Being conservative, make assumes that any change in the header file requires recompilation of all dependent files, but you know that they do not need to be recompiled and you would rather not waste the time waiting for them to compile.

If you anticipate the problem before changing the header file, you can use the '-t' flag. This flag tells make not to run the commands in the rules, but rather to mark the target up to date by changing its last-modification date. You would follow this procedure:

1. Use the command 'make' to recompile the source files that really need recompilation.

2. Make the changes in the header files.

3. Use the command 'make -t' to mark all the object files as up to date. The next time you run make, the changes in the header files will not cause any recompilation.

If you have already changed the header file at a time when some files do need recompilation, it is too late to do this. Instead, you can use the '-o file' flag, which marks a specified file as "old" (see Section 9.7 [Summary of Options], page 89). This means that the file itself will not be remade, and nothing else will be remade on its account. Follow this procedure:

1. Recompile the source files that need compilation for reasons independent of the particular header file, with 'make -o headerfile'. If several header files are involved, use a separate '-o' option for each header file.

2. Touch all the object files with 'make -t'.

9.5 Overriding Variables

An argument that contains '=' specifies the value of a variable: 'v=x' sets the value of the variable v to x. If you specify a value in this way, all ordinary assignments of the same variable in the makefile are ignored; we say they have been *overridden* by the command line argument.

The most common way to use this facility is to pass extra flags to compilers. For example, in a properly written makefile, the variable CFLAGS is included in each command that runs the C compiler, so a file 'foo.c' would be compiled something like this:

```
cc -c $(CFLAGS) foo.c
```
Thus, whatever value you set for CFLAGS affects each compilation that occurs. The makefile probably specifies the usual value for CFLAGS, like this:
```
CFLAGS=-g
```
Each time you run make, you can override this value if you wish. For example, if you say 'make CFLAGS='-g -O'', each C compilation will be done with 'cc -c -g -O'. (This illustrates how you can use quoting in the shell to enclose spaces and other special characters in the value of a variable when you override it.)

The variable CFLAGS is only one of many standard variables that exist just so that you can change them this way. See Section 10.3 [Variables Used by Implicit Rules], page 100, for a complete list.

You can also program the makefile to look at additional variables of your own, giving the user the ability to control other aspects of how the makefile works by changing the variables.

When you override a variable with a command argument, you can define either a recursively-expanded variable or a simply-expanded variable. The examples shown above make a recursively-expanded variable; to make a simply-expanded variable, write ':=' instead of '='. But, unless you want to include a variable reference or function call in the *value* that you specify, it makes no difference which kind of variable you create.

There is one way that the makefile can change a variable that you have overridden. This is to use the override directive, which is a line that looks like this: 'override *variable* = *value*' (see Section 6.7 [The override Directive], page 61).

9.6 Testing the Compilation of a Program

Normally, when an error happens in executing a shell command, make gives up immediately, returning a nonzero status. No further commands are executed for any target. The error implies that the goal cannot be correctly remade, and make reports this as soon as it knows.

When you are compiling a program that you have just changed, this is not what you want. Instead, you would rather that make try compiling every file that can be tried, to show you as many compilation errors as possible.

On these occasions, you should use the '-k' or '--keep-going' flag. This tells make to continue to consider the other dependencies of the pending targets, remaking them if necessary, before it gives up and returns nonzero status. For example, after an error in compiling one object file, 'make -k' will continue compiling other object files even though it already knows that linking them will be impossible. In addition to continuing after failed shell commands, 'make -k' will continue as much as possible after discovering that it does not know how to make a target or dependency file. This will always cause an error message, but without '-k', it is a fatal error (see Section 9.7 [Summary of Options], page 89).

The usual behavior of make assumes that your purpose is to get the goals up to date; once make learns that this is impossible, it might as well report the failure immediately. The '-k' flag says that the real purpose is to test as much as possible of the changes made in the program, perhaps to find several independent problems so that you can correct them all before the next attempt to compile. This is why Emacs' *M-x compile* command passes the '-k' flag by default.

9.7 Summary of Options

Here is a table of all the options make understands:

'-b'

'-m'   These options are ignored for compatibility with other versions of make.

'-C *dir*'

'--directory=*dir*'
                    Change to directory *dir* before reading the makefiles. If multiple '-C' options are specified, each is interpreted relative to the previous one: '-C / -C etc' is equivalent to '-C /etc'. This is typically used with recursive invocations of make (see Section 5.6 [Recursive Use of make], page 42).

'-d'

'--debug'
                    Print debugging information in addition to normal processing. The debugging information says which files are being considered for remaking, which file-times are being compared and with what results, which files actually need to be remade, which implicit rules are considered and which are applied—everything interesting about how make decides what to do.

'-e'

'--environment-overrides'
                    Give variables taken from the environment precedence over variables from makefiles. See Section 6.9 [Variables from the Environment], page 62.

'-f *file*'

'--file=*file*'

'--makefile=*file*'
                    Read the file named *file* as a makefile. See Chapter 3 [Writing Makefiles], page 11.

'-h'
'--help'

> Remind you of the options that make understands and then exit.

'-i'
'--ignore-errors'

> Ignore all errors in commands executed to remake files. See
> Section 5.4 [Errors in Commands], page 40.

'-I *dir*'
'--include-dir=*dir*'

> Specifies a directory *dir* to search for included makefiles. See
> Section 3.3 [Including Other Makefiles], page 12. If several '-I'
> options are used to specify several directories, the directories are
> searched in the order specified.

'-j [*jobs*]'
'--jobs=[*jobs*]'

> Specifies the number of jobs (commands) to run simultaneously.
> With no argument, make runs as many jobs simultaneously as
> possible. If there is more than one '-j' option, the last one is
> effective. See Section 5.3 [Parallel Execution], page 39, for more
> information on how commands are run. Note that this option is
> ignored on MS-DOS.

'-k'
'--keep-going'

> Continue as much as possible after an error. While the target
> that failed, and those that depend on it, cannot be remade,
> the other dependencies of these targets can be processed all the
> same. See Section 9.6 [Testing the Compilation of a Program],
> page 88.

'-l [*load*]'
'--load-average[=*load*]'
'--max-load[=*load*]'

> Specifies that no new jobs (commands) should be started if there
> are other jobs running and the load average is at least *load* (a
> floating-point number). With no argument, removes a previous
> load limit. See Section 5.3 [Parallel Execution], page 39.

'-n'
'--just-print'
'--dry-run'
'--recon'

> Print the commands that would be executed, but do not execute
> them. See Section 9.3 [Instead of Executing the Commands],
> page 85.

'`-o` *file*'
'`--old-file=`*file*'
'`--assume-old=`*file*'

> Do not remake the file *file* even if it is older than its dependencies, and do not remake anything on account of changes in *file*. Essentially the file is treated as very old and its rules are ignored. See Section 9.4 [Avoiding Recompilation of Some Files], page 87.

'`-p`'
'`--print-data-base`'

> Print the data base (rules and variable values) that results from reading the makefiles; then execute as usual or as otherwise specified. This also prints the version information given by the '`-v`' switch (see below). To print the data base without trying to remake any files, use '`make -p -f /dev/null`'.

'`-q`'
'`--question`'

> "Question mode". Do not run any commands, or print anything; just return an exit status that is zero if the specified targets are already up to date, one if any remaking is required, or two if an error is encountered. See Section 9.3 [Instead of Executing the Commands], page 85.

'`-r`'
'`--no-builtin-rules`'

> Eliminate use of the built-in implicit rules (see Chapter 10 [Using Implicit Rules], page 95). You can still define your own by writing pattern rules (see Section 10.5 [Defining and Redefining Pattern Rules], page 103). The '`-r`' option also clears out the default list of suffixes for suffix rules (see Section 10.7 [Old-Fashioned Suffix Rules], page 111). But you can still define your own suffixes with a rule for `.SUFFIXES`, and then define your own suffix rules. Note that only *rules* are affected by the `-r` option; default variables remain in effect (see Section 10.3 [Variables Used by Implicit Rules], page 100).

'`-s`'
'`--silent`'
'`--quiet`'

> Silent operation; do not print the commands as they are executed. See Section 5.1 [Command Echoing], page 37.

'`-S`'
'`--no-keep-going`'
'`--stop`'

Cancel the effect of the '-k' option. This is never necessary except in a recursive make where '-k' might be inherited from the top-level make via MAKEFLAGS (see Section 5.6 [Recursive Use of make], page 42) or if you set '-k' in MAKEFLAGS in your environment.

'-t'
'--touch'

Touch files (mark them up to date without really changing them) instead of running their commands. This is used to pretend that the commands were done, in order to fool future invocations of make. See Section 9.3 [Instead of Executing the Commands], page 85.

'-v'
'--version'

Print the version of the make program plus a copyright, a list of authors, and a notice that there is no warranty; then exit.

'-w'
'--print-directory'

Print a message containing the working directory both before and after executing the makefile. This may be useful for tracking down errors from complicated nests of recursive make commands. See Section 5.6 [Recursive Use of make], page 42. (In practice, you rarely need to specify this option since 'make' does it for you; see Section 5.6.4 [The '--print-directory' Option], page 47.)

'--no-print-directory'

Disable printing of the working directory under -w. This option is useful when -w is turned on automatically, but you do not want to see the extra messages. See Section 5.6.4 [The '--print-directory' Option], page 47.

'-W file'
'--what-if=file'
'--new-file=file'
'--assume-new=file'

Pretend that the target file has just been modified. When used with the '-n' flag, this shows you what would happen if you were to modify that file. Without '-n', it is almost the same as running a touch command on the given file before running make, except that the modification time is changed only in the imagination of make. See Section 9.3 [Instead of Executing the Commands], page 85.

'`--warn-undefined-variables`'

> Issue a warning message whenever `make` sees a reference to an undefined variable. This can be helpful when you are trying to debug makefiles which use variables in complex ways.

10 Using Implicit Rules

Certain standard ways of remaking target files are used very often. For example, one customary way to make an object file is from a C source file using the C compiler, `cc`.

Implicit rules tell **make** how to use customary techniques so that you do not have to specify them in detail when you want to use them. For example, there is an implicit rule for C compilation. File names determine which implicit rules are run. For example, C compilation typically takes a '.c' file and makes a '.o' file. So **make** applies the implicit rule for C compilation when it sees this combination of file name endings.

A chain of implicit rules can apply in sequence; for example, **make** will remake a '.o' file from a '.y' file by way of a '.c' file. See Section 10.4 [Chains of Implicit Rules], page 102.

The built-in implicit rules use several variables in their commands so that, by changing the values of the variables, you can change the way the implicit rule works. For example, the variable **CFLAGS** controls the flags given to the C compiler by the implicit rule for C compilation. See Section 10.3 [Variables Used by Implicit Rules], page 100.

You can define your own implicit rules by writing *pattern rules*. See Section 10.5 [Defining and Redefining Pattern Rules], page 103.

Suffix rules are a more limited way to define implicit rules. Pattern rules are more general and clearer, but suffix rules are retained for compatibility. See Section 10.7 [Old-Fashioned Suffix Rules], page 111.

10.1 Using Implicit Rules

To allow **make** to find a customary method for updating a target file, all you have to do is refrain from specifying commands yourself. Either write a rule with no command lines, or don't write a rule at all. Then **make** will figure out which implicit rule to use based on which kind of source file exists or can be made.

For example, suppose the makefile looks like this:

```
foo : foo.o bar.o
        cc -o foo foo.o bar.o $(CFLAGS) $(LDFLAGS)
```

Because you mention 'foo.o' but do not give a rule for it, **make** will automatically look for an implicit rule that tells how to update it. This happens whether or not the file 'foo.o' currently exists.

If an implicit rule is found, it can supply both commands and one or more dependencies (the source files). You would want to write a rule for 'foo.o' with no command lines if you need to specify additional dependencies, such as header files, that the implicit rule cannot supply.

Each implicit rule has a target pattern and dependency patterns. There may be many implicit rules with the same target pattern. For example, numerous rules make '.o' files: one, from a '.c' file with the C compiler; another, from a '.p' file with the Pascal compiler; and so on. The rule that actually applies is the one whose dependencies exist or can be made. So, if you have a file 'foo.c', make will run the C compiler; otherwise, if you have a file 'foo.p', make will run the Pascal compiler; and so on.

Of course, when you write the makefile, you know which implicit rule you want make to use, and you know it will choose that one because you know which possible dependency files are supposed to exist. See Section 10.2 [Catalogue of Implicit Rules], page 96, for a catalogue of all the predefined implicit rules.

Above, we said an implicit rule applies if the required dependencies "exist or can be made". A file "can be made" if it is mentioned explicitly in the makefile as a target or a dependency, or if an implicit rule can be recursively found for how to make it. When an implicit dependency is the result of another implicit rule, we say that *chaining* is occurring. See Section 10.4 [Chains of Implicit Rules], page 102.

In general, make searches for an implicit rule for each target, and for each double-colon rule, that has no commands. A file that is mentioned only as a dependency is considered a target whose rule specifies nothing, so implicit rule search happens for it. See Section 10.8 [Implicit Rule Search Algorithm], page 112, for the details of how the search is done.

Note that explicit dependencies do not influence implicit rule search. For example, consider this explicit rule:

```
foo.o: foo.p
```

The dependency on 'foo.p' does not necessarily mean that make will remake 'foo.o' according to the implicit rule to make an object file, a '.o' file, from a Pascal source file, a '.p' file. For example, if 'foo.c' also exists, the implicit rule to make an object file from a C source file is used instead, because it appears before the Pascal rule in the list of predefined implicit rules (see Section 10.2 [Catalogue of Implicit Rules], page 96).

If you do not want an implicit rule to be used for a target that has no commands, you can give that target empty commands by writing a semicolon (see Section 5.8 [Defining Empty Commands], page 49).

10.2 Catalogue of Implicit Rules

Here is a catalogue of predefined implicit rules which are always available unless the makefile explicitly overrides or cancels them. See Section 10.5.6 [Canceling Implicit Rules], page 110, for information on canceling or overriding an implicit rule. The '-r' or '--no-builtin-rules' option cancels all predefined rules.

Not all of these rules will always be defined, even when the '-r' option is not given. Many of the predefined implicit rules are implemented in make as suffix rules, so which ones will be defined depends on the *suffix list* (the list of dependencies of the special target .SUFFIXES). The default suffix list is: .out, .a, .ln, .o, .c, .cc, .C, .p, .f, .F, .r, .y, .l, .s, .S, .mod, .sym, .def, .h, .info, .dvi, .tex, .texinfo, .texi, .txinfo, .w, .ch .web, .sh, .elc, .el. All of the implicit rules described below whose dependencies have one of these suffixes are actually suffix rules. If you modify the suffix list, the only predefined suffix rules in effect will be those named by one or two of the suffixes that are on the list you specify; rules whose suffixes fail to be on the list are disabled. See Section 10.7 [Old-Fashioned Suffix Rules], page 111, for full details on suffix rules.

Compiling C programs
> '*n*.o' is made automatically from '*n*.c' with a command of the form '$(CC) -c $(CPPFLAGS) $(CFLAGS)'.

Compiling C++ programs
> '*n*.o' is made automatically from '*n*.cc' or '*n*.C' with a command of the form '$(CXX) -c $(CPPFLAGS) $(CXXFLAGS)'. We encourage you to use the suffix '.cc' for C++ source files instead of '.C'.

Compiling Pascal programs
> '*n*.o' is made automatically from '*n*.p' with the command '$(PC) -c $(PFLAGS)'.

Compiling Fortran and Ratfor programs
> '*n*.o' is made automatically from '*n*.r', '*n*.F' or '*n*.f' by running the Fortran compiler. The precise command used is as follows:
>
> | '.f' | '$(FC) -c $(FFLAGS)'. |
> |------|----------------------|
> | '.F' | '$(FC) -c $(FFLAGS) $(CPPFLAGS)'. |
> | '.r' | '$(FC) -c $(FFLAGS) $(RFLAGS)'. |

Preprocessing Fortran and Ratfor programs
> '*n*.f' is made automatically from '*n*.r' or '*n*.F'. This rule runs just the preprocessor to convert a Ratfor or preprocessable Fortran program into a strict Fortran program. The precise command used is as follows:
>
> | '.F' | '$(FC) -F $(CPPFLAGS) $(FFLAGS)'. |
> |------|----------------------------------|
> | '.r' | '$(FC) -F $(FFLAGS) $(RFLAGS)'. |

Compiling Modula-2 programs
> '*n*.sym' is made from '*n*.def' with a command of the form '$(M2C) $(M2FLAGS) $(DEFFLAGS)'. '*n*.o' is made from '*n*.mod'; the form is: '$(M2C) $(M2FLAGS) $(MODFLAGS)'.

Assembling and preprocessing assembler programs

'*n*.o' is made automatically from '*n*.s' by running the assembler, `as`. The precise command is '`$(AS) $(ASFLAGS)`'.

'*n*.s' is made automatically from '*n*.S' by running the C preprocessor, `cpp`. The precise command is '`$(CPP) $(CPPFLAGS)`'.

Linking a single object file

'*n*' is made automatically from '*n*.o' by running the linker (usually called `ld`) via the C compiler. The precise command used is '`$(CC) $(LDFLAGS) `*n*`.o $(LOADLIBES)`'.

This rule does the right thing for a simple program with only one source file. It will also do the right thing if there are multiple object files (presumably coming from various other source files), one of which has a name matching that of the executable file. Thus,

```
x: y.o z.o
```

when '`x.c`', '`y.c`' and '`z.c`' all exist will execute:

```
cc -c x.c -o x.o
cc -c y.c -o y.o
cc -c z.c -o z.o
cc x.o y.o z.o -o x
rm -f x.o
rm -f y.o
rm -f z.o
```

In more complicated cases, such as when there is no object file whose name derives from the executable file name, you must write an explicit command for linking.

Each kind of file automatically made into '.o' object files will be automatically linked by using the compiler ('`$(CC)`', '`$(FC)`' or '`$(PC)`'; the C compiler '`$(CC)`' is used to assemble '.s' files) without the '-c' option. This could be done by using the '.o' object files as intermediates, but it is faster to do the compiling and linking in one step, so that's how it's done.

Yacc for C programs

'*n*.c' is made automatically from '*n*.y' by running Yacc with the command '`$(YACC) $(YFLAGS)`'.

Lex for C programs

'*n*.c' is made automatically from '*n*.l' by by running Lex. The actual command is '`$(LEX) $(LFLAGS)`'.

Lex for Ratfor programs
: 'n.r' is made automatically from 'n.l' by by running Lex. The actual command is '$(LEX) $(LFLAGS)'.

  The convention of using the same suffix '.l' for all Lex files regardless of whether they produce C code or Ratfor code makes it impossible for make to determine automatically which of the two languages you are using in any particular case. If make is called upon to remake an object file from a '.l' file, it must guess which compiler to use. It will guess the C compiler, because that is more common. If you are using Ratfor, make sure make knows this by mentioning 'n.r' in the makefile. Or, if you are using Ratfor exclusively, with no C files, remove '.c' from the list of implicit rule suffixes with:

```
.SUFFIXES:
.SUFFIXES: .o .r .f .l ...
```

Making Lint Libraries from C, Yacc, or Lex programs
: 'n.ln' is made from 'n.c' by running lint. The precise command is '$(LINT) $(LINTFLAGS) $(CPPFLAGS) -i'. The same command is used on the C code produced from 'n.y' or 'n.l'.

TEX and Web
: 'n.dvi' is made from 'n.tex' with the command '$(TEX)'. '$n$.tex' is made from '$n$.web' with '$(WEAVE)', or from 'n.w' (and from 'n.ch' if it exists or can be made) with '$(CWEAVE)'. '$n$.p' is made from '$n$.web' with '$(TANGLE)' and 'n.c' is made from 'n.w' (and from 'n.ch' if it exists or can be made) with '$(CTANGLE)'.

Texinfo and Info
: 'n.dvi' is made from 'n.texinfo', 'n.texi', or 'n.txinfo', with the command '$(TEXI2DVI) $(TEXI2DVI_FLAGS)'. '$n$.info' is made from '$n$.texinfo', '$n$.texi', or '$n$.txinfo', with the command '$(MAKEINFO) $(MAKEINFO_FLAGS)'.

RCS
: Any file 'n' is extracted if necessary from an RCS file named either 'n,v' or 'RCS/n,v'. The precise command used is '$(CO) $(COFLAGS)'. '$n$' will not be extracted from RCS if it already exists, even if the RCS file is newer. The rules for RCS are terminal (see Section 10.5.5 [Match-Anything Pattern Rules], page 109), so RCS files cannot be generated from another source; they must actually exist.

SCCS
: Any file 'n' is extracted if necessary from an SCCS file named either 's.n' or 'SCCS/s.n'. The precise command used is '$(GET) $(GFLAGS)'. The rules for SCCS are terminal (see Section 10.5.5 [Match-Anything Pattern Rules], page 109), so SCCS

files cannot be generated from another source; they must actually exist.

For the benefit of SCCS, a file 'n' is copied from 'n.sh' and made executable (by everyone). This is for shell scripts that are checked into SCCS. Since RCS preserves the execution permission of a file, you do not need to use this feature with RCS.

We recommend that you avoid using of SCCS. RCS is widely held to be superior, and is also free. By choosing free software in place of comparable (or inferior) proprietary software, you support the free software movement.

Usually, you want to change only the variables listed in the table above, which are documented in the following section.

However, the commands in built-in implicit rules actually use variables such as COMPILE.c, LINK.p, and PREPROCESS.S, whose values contain the commands listed above.

make follows the convention that the rule to compile a '.x' source file uses the variable COMPILE.x. Similarly, the rule to produce an executable from a '.x' file uses LINK.x; and the rule to preprocess a '.x' file uses PREPROCESS.x.

Every rule that produces an object file uses the variable OUTPUT_OPTION. make defines this variable either to contain '-o $@', or to be empty, depending on a compile-time option. You need the '-o' option to ensure that the output goes into the right file when the source file is in a different directory, as when using VPATH (see Section 4.3 [Directory Search], page 21). However, compilers on some systems do not accept a '-o' switch for object files. If you use such a system, and use VPATH, some compilations will put their output in the wrong place. A possible workaround for this problem is to give OUTPUT_OPTION the value '; mv $*.o $@'.

10.3 Variables Used by Implicit Rules

The commands in built-in implicit rules make liberal use of certain predefined variables. You can alter these variables in the makefile, with arguments to make, or in the environment to alter how the implicit rules work without redefining the rules themselves.

For example, the command used to compile a C source file actually says '$(CC) -c $(CFLAGS) $(CPPFLAGS)'. The default values of the variables used are 'cc' and nothing, resulting in the command 'cc -c'. By redefining 'CC' to 'ncc', you could cause 'ncc' to be used for all C compilations performed by the implicit rule. By redefining 'CFLAGS' to be '-g', you could pass the '-g' option to each compilation. *All* implicit rules that do C compilation use '$(CC)' to get the program name for the compiler and *all* include '$(CFLAGS)' among the arguments given to the compiler.

The variables used in implicit rules fall into two classes: those that are names of programs (like CC) and those that contain arguments for the programs (like CFLAGS). (The "name of a program" may also contain some command arguments, but it must start with an actual executable program name.) If a variable value contains more than one argument, separate them with spaces.

Here is a table of variables used as names of programs in built-in rules:

AR   Archive-maintaining program; default 'ar'.

AS   Program for doing assembly; default 'as'.

CC   Program for compiling C programs; default 'cc'.

CXX   Program for compiling C++ programs; default 'g++'.

CO   Program for extracting a file from RCS; default 'co'.

CPP   Program for running the C preprocessor, with results to standard output; default '$(CC) -E'.

FC   Program for compiling or preprocessing Fortran and Ratfor programs; default 'f77'.

GET   Program for extracting a file from SCCS; default 'get'.

LEX   Program to use to turn Lex grammars into C programs or Ratfor programs; default 'lex'.

PC   Program for compiling Pascal programs; default 'pc'.

YACC   Program to use to turn Yacc grammars into C programs; default 'yacc'.

YACCR   Program to use to turn Yacc grammars into Ratfor programs; default 'yacc -r'.

MAKEINFO   Program to convert a Texinfo source file into an Info file; default 'makeinfo'.

TEX   Program to make TeX DVI files from TeX source; default 'tex'.

TEXI2DVI   Program to make TeX DVI files from Texinfo source; default 'texi2dvi'.

WEAVE   Program to translate Web into TeX; default 'weave'.

CWEAVE   Program to translate C Web into TeX; default 'cweave'.

TANGLE   Program to translate Web into Pascal; default 'tangle'.

CTANGLE   Program to translate C Web into C; default 'ctangle'.

RM   Command to remove a file; default 'rm -f'.

Here is a table of variables whose values are additional arguments for the programs above. The default values for all of these is the empty string, unless otherwise noted.

ARFLAGS   Flags to give the archive-maintaining program; default '`rv`'.

ASFLAGS   Extra flags to give to the assembler (when explicitly invoked on a '`.s`' or '`.S`' file).

CFLAGS   Extra flags to give to the C compiler.

CXXFLAGS   Extra flags to give to the C++ compiler.

COFLAGS   Extra flags to give to the RCS `co` program.

CPPFLAGS   Extra flags to give to the C preprocessor and programs that use it (the C and Fortran compilers).

FFLAGS   Extra flags to give to the Fortran compiler.

GFLAGS   Extra flags to give to the SCCS `get` program.

LDFLAGS   Extra flags to give to compilers when they are supposed to invoke the linker, '`ld`'.

LFLAGS   Extra flags to give to Lex.

PFLAGS   Extra flags to give to the Pascal compiler.

RFLAGS   Extra flags to give to the Fortran compiler for Ratfor programs.

YFLAGS   Extra flags to give to Yacc.

10.4 Chains of Implicit Rules

Sometimes a file can be made by a sequence of implicit rules. For example, a file '`n.o`' could be made from '`n.y`' by running first Yacc and then `cc`. Such a sequence is called a *chain*.

If the file '`n.c`' exists, or is mentioned in the makefile, no special searching is required: `make` finds that the object file can be made by C compilation from '`n.c`'; later on, when considering how to make '`n.c`', the rule for running Yacc is used. Ultimately both '`n.c`' and '`n.o`' are updated.

However, even if '`n.c`' does not exist and is not mentioned, `make` knows how to envision it as the missing link between '`n.o`' and '`n.y`'! In this case, '`n.c`' is called an *intermediate file*. Once `make` has decided to use the intermediate file, it is entered in the data base as if it had been mentioned in the makefile, along with the implicit rule that says how to create it.

Intermediate files are remade using their rules just like all other files. But intermediate files are treated differently in two ways.

The first difference is what happens if the intermediate file does not exist. If an ordinary file b does not exist, and `make` considers a target that depends on b, it invariably creates b and then updates the target from b. But if b is an intermediate file, then **make** can leave well enough alone. It won't bother updating b, or the ultimate target, unless some dependency of b is newer than that target or there is some other reason to update that target.

The second difference is that if **make** *does* create b in order to update something else, it deletes b later on after it is no longer needed. Therefore, an intermediate file which did not exist before **make** also does not exist after **make**. **make** reports the deletion to you by printing a 'rm -f' command showing which file it is deleting.

Ordinarily, a file cannot be intermediate if it is mentioned in the makefile as a target or dependency. However, you can explicitly mark a file as intermediate by listing it as a dependency of the special target .INTERMEDIATE. This takes effect even if the file is mentioned explicitly in some other way.

You can prevent automatic deletion of an intermediate file by marking it as a *secondary* file. To do this, list it as a dependency of the special target .SECONDARY. When a file is secondary, **make** will not create the file merely because it does not already exist, but **make** does not automatically delete the file. Marking a file as secondary also marks it as intermediate.

You can list the target pattern of an implicit rule (such as '%.o') as a dependency of the special target .PRECIOUS to preserve intermediate files made by implicit rules whose target patterns match that file's name; see Section 5.5 [Interrupts], page 42.

A chain can involve more than two implicit rules. For example, it is possible to make a file 'foo' from 'RCS/foo.y,v' by running RCS, Yacc and cc. Then both 'foo.y' and 'foo.c' are intermediate files that are deleted at the end.

No single implicit rule can appear more than once in a chain. This means that **make** will not even consider such a ridiculous thing as making 'foo' from 'foo.o.o' by running the linker twice. This constraint has the added benefit of preventing any infinite loop in the search for an implicit rule chain.

There are some special implicit rules to optimize certain cases that would otherwise be handled by rule chains. For example, making 'foo' from 'foo.c' could be handled by compiling and linking with separate chained rules, using 'foo.o' as an intermediate file. But what actually happens is that a special rule for this case does the compilation and linking with a single cc command. The optimized rule is used in preference to the step-by-step chain because it comes earlier in the ordering of rules.

10.5 Defining and Redefining Pattern Rules

You define an implicit rule by writing a *pattern rule*. A pattern rule looks like an ordinary rule, except that its target contains the character '%' (exactly one of them). The target is considered a pattern for matching file names; the '%' can match any nonempty substring, while other characters match only themselves. The dependencies likewise use '%' to show how their names relate to the target name.

Thus, a pattern rule '%.o : %.c' says how to make any file 'stem.o' from another file 'stem.c'.

Note that expansion using '%' in pattern rules occurs **after** any variable or function expansions, which take place when the makefile is read. See Chapter 6 [How to Use Variables], page 51, and Chapter 8 [Functions for Transforming Text], page 71.

10.5.1 Introduction to Pattern Rules

A pattern rule contains the character '%' (exactly one of them) in the target; otherwise, it looks exactly like an ordinary rule. The target is a pattern for matching file names; the '%' matches any nonempty substring, while other characters match only themselves.

For example, '%.c' as a pattern matches any file name that ends in '.c'. 's.%.c' as a pattern matches any file name that starts with 's.', ends in '.c' and is at least five characters long. (There must be at least one character to match the '%'.) The substring that the '%' matches is called the *stem*.

'%' in a dependency of a pattern rule stands for the same stem that was matched by the '%' in the target. In order for the pattern rule to apply, its target pattern must match the file name under consideration, and its dependency patterns must name files that exist or can be made. These files become dependencies of the target.

Thus, a rule of the form

    %.o : %.c ; *command*...

specifies how to make a file 'n.o', with another file 'n.c' as its dependency, provided that 'n.c' exists or can be made.

There may also be dependencies that do not use '%'; such a dependency attaches to every file made by this pattern rule. These unvarying dependencies are useful occasionally.

A pattern rule need not have any dependencies that contain '%', or in fact any dependencies at all. Such a rule is effectively a general wildcard. It provides a way to make any file that matches the target pattern. See Section 10.6 [Last Resort], page 110.

Pattern rules may have more than one target. Unlike normal rules, this does not act as many different rules with the same dependencies and commands. If a pattern rule has multiple targets, make knows that the rule's commands are responsible for making all of the targets. The commands are executed only once to make all the targets. When searching for a pattern rule to match a target, the target patterns of a rule other than the one that matches the target in need of a rule are incidental: make worries only about giving commands and dependencies to the file presently in question. However, when this file's commands are run, the other targets are marked as having been updated themselves.

The order in which pattern rules appear in the makefile is important since this is the order in which they are considered. Of equally applicable rules, only the first one found is used. The rules you write take precedence over those that are built in. Note however, that a rule whose dependencies actually exist or are mentioned always takes priority over a rule with dependencies that must be made by chaining other implicit rules.

10.5.2 Pattern Rule Examples

Here are some examples of pattern rules actually predefined in `make`. First, the rule that compiles '`.c`' files into '`.o`' files:

```
%.o : %.c
        $(CC) -c $(CFLAGS) $(CPPFLAGS) $< -o $@
```

defines a rule that can make any file '`x.o`' from '`x.c`'. The command uses the automatic variables '`$@`' and '`$<`' to substitute the names of the target file and the source file in each case where the rule applies (see Section 10.5.3 [Automatic Variables], page 106).

Here is a second built-in rule:

```
% :: RCS/%,v
        $(CO) $(COFLAGS) $<
```

defines a rule that can make any file '`x`' whatsoever from a corresponding file '`x,v`' in the subdirectory '`RCS`'. Since the target is '`%`', this rule will apply to any file whatever, provided the appropriate dependency file exists. The double colon makes the rule *terminal*, which means that its dependency may not be an intermediate file (see Section 10.5.5 [Match-Anything Pattern Rules], page 109).

This pattern rule has two targets:

```
%.tab.c %.tab.h: %.y
        bison -d $<
```

This tells `make` that the command '`bison -d x.y`' will make both '`x.tab.c`' and '`x.tab.h`'. If the file '`foo`' depends on the files '`parse.tab.o`' and '`scan.o`' and the file '`scan.o`' depends on the file '`parse.tab.h`', when '`parse.y`' is changed, the command '`bison -d parse.y`' will be executed only once, and the dependencies of both '`parse.tab.o`' and '`scan.o`' will be satisfied. (Presumably the file '`parse.tab.o`' will be recompiled from '`parse.tab.c`' and the file '`scan.o`' from '`scan.c`', while '`foo`' is linked from '`parse.tab.o`', '`scan.o`', and its other dependencies, and it will execute happily ever after.)

10.5.3 Automatic Variables

Suppose you are writing a pattern rule to compile a '.c' file into a '.o' file: how do you write the 'cc' command so that it operates on the right source file name? You cannot write the name in the command, because the name is different each time the implicit rule is applied.

What you do is use a special feature of make, the *automatic variables*. These variables have values computed afresh for each rule that is executed, based on the target and dependencies of the rule. In this example, you would use '$@' for the object file name and '$<' for the source file name.

Here is a table of automatic variables:

$@   The file name of the target of the rule. If the target is an archive member, then '$@' is the name of the archive file. In a pattern rule that has multiple targets (see Section 10.5.1 [Introduction to Pattern Rules], page 104), '$@' is the name of whichever target caused the rule's commands to be run.

$%   The target member name, when the target is an archive member. See Chapter 11 [Archives], page 115. For example, if the target is 'foo.a(bar.o)' then '$%' is 'bar.o' and '$@' is 'foo.a'. '$%' is empty when the target is not an archive member.

$<   The name of the first dependency. If the target got its commands from an implicit rule, this will be the first dependency added by the implicit rule (see Chapter 10 [Implicit Rules], page 95).

$?   The names of all the dependencies that are newer than the target, with spaces between them. For dependencies which are archive members, only the member named is used (see Chapter 11 [Archives], page 115).

$^   The names of all the dependencies, with spaces between them. For dependencies which are archive members, only the member named is used (see Chapter 11 [Archives], page 115). A target has only one dependency on each other file it depends on, no matter how many times each file is listed as a dependency. So if you list a dependency more than once for a target, the value of $^ contains just one copy of the name.

$+   This is like '$^', but dependencies listed more than once are duplicated in the order they were listed in the makefile. This is primarily useful for use in linking commands where it is meaningful to repeat library file names in a particular order.

$*   The stem with which an implicit rule matches (see Section 10.5.4 [How Patterns Match], page 108). If the target is 'dir/a.foo.b' and the target pattern is 'a.%.b' then the stem is 'dir/foo'. The stem is useful for constructing names of related files.

In a static pattern rule, the stem is part of the file name that matched the '%' in the target pattern.

In an explicit rule, there is no stem; so '$*' cannot be determined in that way. Instead, if the target name ends with a recognized suffix (see Section 10.7 [Old-Fashioned Suffix Rules], page 111), '$*' is set to the target name minus the suffix. For example, if the target name is 'foo.c', then '$*' is set to 'foo', since '.c' is a suffix. GNU make does this bizarre thing only for compatibility with other implementations of make. You should generally avoid using '$*' except in implicit rules or static pattern rules.

If the target name in an explicit rule does not end with a recognized suffix, '$*' is set to the empty string for that rule.

'$?' is useful even in explicit rules when you wish to operate on only the dependencies that have changed. For example, suppose that an archive named 'lib' is supposed to contain copies of several object files. This rule copies just the changed object files into the archive:

```
lib: foo.o bar.o lose.o win.o
        ar r lib $?
```

Of the variables listed above, four have values that are single file names, and two have values that are lists of file names. These six have variants that get just the file's directory name or just the file name within the directory. The variant variables' names are formed by appending 'D' or 'F', respectively. These variants are semi-obsolete in GNU make since the functions dir and notdir can be used to get a similar effect (see Section 8.3 [Functions for File Names], page 75). Note, however, that the 'F' variants all omit the trailing slash which always appears in the output of the dir function. Here is a table of the variants:

'$(@D)'   The directory part of the file name of the target, with the trailing slash removed. If the value of '$@' is 'dir/foo.o' then '$(@D)' is 'dir'. This value is '.' if '$@' does not contain a slash.

'$(@F)'   The file-within-directory part of the file name of the target. If the value of '$@' is 'dir/foo.o' then '$(@F)' is 'foo.o'. '$(@F)' is equivalent to '$(notdir $@)'.

'$(*D)'
'$(*F)'   The directory part and the file-within-directory part of the stem; 'dir' and 'foo' in this example.

'$(%D)'
'$(%F)'   The directory part and the file-within-directory part of the target archive member name. This makes sense only for archive

member targets of the form 'archive(member)' and is useful only when member may contain a directory name. (See Section 11.1 [Archive Members as Targets], page 115.)

'$(<D)'

'$(<F)'   The directory part and the file-within-directory part of the first dependency.

'$(^D)'

'$(^F)'   Lists of the directory parts and the file-within-directory parts of all dependencies.

'$(?D)'

'$(?F)'   Lists of the directory parts and the file-within-directory parts of all dependencies that are newer than the target.

Note that we use a special stylistic convention when we talk about these automatic variables; we write "the value of '$<'", rather than "the variable <" as we would write for ordinary variables such as objects and CFLAGS. We think this convention looks more natural in this special case. Please do not assume it has a deep significance; '$<' refers to the variable named < just as '$(CFLAGS)' refers to the variable named CFLAGS. You could just as well use '$(<)' in place of '$<'.

10.5.4 How Patterns Match

A target pattern is composed of a '%' between a prefix and a suffix, either or both of which may be empty. The pattern matches a file name only if the file name starts with the prefix and ends with the suffix, without overlap. The text between the prefix and the suffix is called the *stem*. Thus, when the pattern '%.o' matches the file name 'test.o', the stem is 'test'. The pattern rule dependencies are turned into actual file names by substituting the stem for the character '%'. Thus, if in the same example one of the dependencies is written as '%.c', it expands to 'test.c'.

When the target pattern does not contain a slash (and it usually does not), directory names in the file names are removed from the file name before it is compared with the target prefix and suffix. After the comparison of the file name to the target pattern, the directory names, along with the slash that ends them, are added on to the dependency file names generated from the pattern rule's dependency patterns and the file name. The directories are ignored only for the purpose of finding an implicit rule to use, not in the application of that rule. Thus, 'e%t' matches the file name 'src/eat', with 'src/a' as the stem. When dependencies are turned into file names, the directories from the stem are added at the front, while the rest of the stem is substituted for the '%'. The stem 'src/a' with a dependency pattern 'c%r' gives the file name 'src/car'.

10.5.5 Match-Anything Pattern Rules

When a pattern rule's target is just '%', it matches any file name whatever. We call these rules *match-anything* rules. They are very useful, but it can take a lot of time for **make** to think about them, because it must consider every such rule for each file name listed either as a target or as a dependency.

Suppose the makefile mentions 'foo.c'. For this target, **make** would have to consider making it by linking an object file 'foo.c.o', or by C compilation-and-linking in one step from 'foo.c.c', or by Pascal compilation-and-linking from 'foo.c.p', and many other possibilities.

We know these possibilities are ridiculous since 'foo.c' is a C source file, not an executable. If **make** did consider these possibilities, it would ultimately reject them, because files such as 'foo.c.o' and 'foo.c.p' would not exist. But these possibilities are so numerous that **make** would run very slowly if it had to consider them.

To gain speed, we have put various constraints on the way **make** considers match-anything rules. There are two different constraints that can be applied, and each time you define a match-anything rule you must choose one or the other for that rule.

One choice is to mark the match-anything rule as *terminal* by defining it with a double colon. When a rule is terminal, it does not apply unless its dependencies actually exist. Dependencies that could be made with other implicit rules are not good enough. In other words, no further chaining is allowed beyond a terminal rule.

For example, the built-in implicit rules for extracting sources from RCS and SCCS files are terminal; as a result, if the file 'foo.c,v' does not exist, **make** will not even consider trying to make it as an intermediate file from 'foo.c,v.o' or from 'RCS/SCCS/s.foo.c,v'. RCS and SCCS files are generally ultimate source files, which should not be remade from any other files; therefore, **make** can save time by not looking for ways to remake them.

If you do not mark the match-anything rule as terminal, then it is non-terminal. A nonterminal match-anything rule cannot apply to a file name that indicates a specific type of data. A file name indicates a specific type of data if some non-match-anything implicit rule target matches it.

For example, the file name 'foo.c' matches the target for the pattern rule '%.c : %.y' (the rule to run Yacc). Regardless of whether this rule is actually applicable (which happens only if there is a file 'foo.y'), the fact that its target matches is enough to prevent consideration of any nonterminal match-anything rules for the file 'foo.c'. Thus, **make** will not even consider trying to make 'foo.c' as an executable file from 'foo.c.o', 'foo.c.c', 'foo.c.p', etc.

The motivation for this constraint is that nonterminal match-anything rules are used for making files containing specific types of data (such as executable files) and a file name with a recognized suffix indicates some other specific type of data (such as a C source file).

Special built-in dummy pattern rules are provided solely to recognize certain file names so that nonterminal match-anything rules will not be considered. These dummy rules have no dependencies and no commands, and they are ignored for all other purposes. For example, the built-in implicit rule

```
%.p :
```

exists to make sure that Pascal source files such as 'foo.p' match a specific target pattern and thereby prevent time from being wasted looking for 'foo.p.o' or 'foo.p.c'.

Dummy pattern rules such as the one for '%.p' are made for every suffix listed as valid for use in suffix rules (see Section 10.7 [Old-Fashioned Suffix Rules], page 111).

10.5.6 Canceling Implicit Rules

You can override a built-in implicit rule (or one you have defined yourself) by defining a new pattern rule with the same target and dependencies, but different commands. When the new rule is defined, the built-in one is replaced. The new rule's position in the sequence of implicit rules is determined by where you write the new rule.

You can cancel a built-in implicit rule by defining a pattern rule with the same target and dependencies, but no commands. For example, the following would cancel the rule that runs the assembler:

```
%.o : %.s
```

10.6 Defining Last-Resort Default Rules

You can define a last-resort implicit rule by writing a terminal match-anything pattern rule with no dependencies (see Section 10.5.5 [Match-Anything Rules], page 109). This is just like any other pattern rule; the only thing special about it is that it will match any target. So such a rule's commands are used for all targets and dependencies that have no commands of their own and for which no other implicit rule applies.

For example, when testing a makefile, you might not care if the source files contain real data, only that they exist. Then you might do this:

```
%::
        touch $@
```

to cause all the source files needed (as dependencies) to be created automatically.

You can instead define commands to be used for targets for which there are no rules at all, even ones which don't specify commands. You do this by writing a rule for the target .DEFAULT. Such a rule's commands are used for all dependencies which do not appear as targets in any explicit rule, and for which no implicit rule applies. Naturally, there is no .DEFAULT rule unless you write one.

If you use .DEFAULT with no commands or dependencies:

```
.DEFAULT:
```

the commands previously stored for .DEFAULT are cleared. Then make acts as if you had never defined .DEFAULT at all.

If you do not want a target to get the commands from a match-anything pattern rule or .DEFAULT, but you also do not want any commands to be run for the target, you can give it empty commands (see Section 5.8 [Defining Empty Commands], page 49).

You can use a last-resort rule to override part of another makefile. See Section 3.6 [Overriding Part of Another Makefile], page 15.

10.7 Old-Fashioned Suffix Rules

Suffix rules are the old-fashioned way of defining implicit rules for make. Suffix rules are obsolete because pattern rules are more general and clearer. They are supported in GNU make for compatibility with old makefiles. They come in two kinds: *double-suffix* and *single-suffix*.

A double-suffix rule is defined by a pair of suffixes: the target suffix and the source suffix. It matches any file whose name ends with the target suffix. The corresponding implicit dependency is made by replacing the target suffix with the source suffix in the file name. A two-suffix rule whose target and source suffixes are '.o' and '.c' is equivalent to the pattern rule '%.o : %.c'.

A single-suffix rule is defined by a single suffix, which is the source suffix. It matches any file name, and the corresponding implicit dependency name is made by appending the source suffix. A single-suffix rule whose source suffix is '.c' is equivalent to the pattern rule '% : %.c'.

Suffix rule definitions are recognized by comparing each rule's target against a defined list of known suffixes. When make sees a rule whose target is a known suffix, this rule is considered a single-suffix rule. When make sees a rule whose target is two known suffixes concatenated, this rule is taken as a double-suffix rule.

For example, '.c' and '.o' are both on the default list of known suffixes. Therefore, if you define a rule whose target is '.c.o', make takes it to be a double-suffix rule with source suffix '.c' and target suffix '.o'. Here is the old-fashioned way to define the rule for compiling a C source file:

```
.c.o:
        $(CC) -c $(CFLAGS) $(CPPFLAGS) -o $@ $<
```

Suffix rules cannot have any dependencies of their own. If they have any, they are treated as normal files with funny names, not as suffix rules. Thus, the rule:

```
.c.o: foo.h
        $(CC) -c $(CFLAGS) $(CPPFLAGS) -o $@ $<
```

tells how to make the file '.c.o' from the dependency file 'foo.h', and is not at all like the pattern rule:

```
%.o: %.c foo.h
        $(CC) -c $(CFLAGS) $(CPPFLAGS) -o $@ $<
```

which tells how to make '.o' files from '.c' files, and makes all '.o' files using this pattern rule also depend on 'foo.h'.

Suffix rules with no commands are also meaningless. They do not remove previous rules as do pattern rules with no commands (see Section 10.5.6 [Canceling Implicit Rules], page 110). They simply enter the suffix or pair of suffixes concatenated as a target in the data base.

The known suffixes are simply the names of the dependencies of the special target .SUFFIXES. You can add your own suffixes by writing a rule for .SUFFIXES that adds more dependencies, as in:

```
.SUFFIXES: .hack .win
```

which adds '.hack' and '.win' to the end of the list of suffixes.

If you wish to eliminate the default known suffixes instead of just adding to them, write a rule for .SUFFIXES with no dependencies. By special dispensation, this eliminates all existing dependencies of .SUFFIXES. You can then write another rule to add the suffixes you want. For example,

```
.SUFFIXES:              # Delete the default suffixes
.SUFFIXES: .c .o .h     # Define our suffix list
```

The '-r' or '--no-builtin-rules' flag causes the default list of suffixes to be empty.

The variable SUFFIXES is defined to the default list of suffixes before make reads any makefiles. You can change the list of suffixes with a rule for the special target .SUFFIXES, but that does not alter this variable.

10.8 Implicit Rule Search Algorithm

Here is the procedure make uses for searching for an implicit rule for a target t. This procedure is followed for each double-colon rule with no commands, for each target of ordinary rules none of which have commands, and for each dependency that is not the target of any rule. It is also followed recursively for dependencies that come from implicit rules, in the search for a chain of rules.

Suffix rules are not mentioned in this algorithm because suffix rules are converted to equivalent pattern rules once the makefiles have been read in.

For an archive member target of the form 'archive(member)', the following algorithm is run twice, first using the entire target name t, and second using '(member)' as the target t if the first run found no rule.

1. Split t into a directory part, called d, and the rest, called n. For example, if t is 'src/foo.o', then d is 'src/' and n is 'foo.o'.

2. Make a list of all the pattern rules one of whose targets matches t or n. If the target pattern contains a slash, it is matched against t; otherwise, against n.

3. If any rule in that list is *not* a match-anything rule, then remove all nonterminal match-anything rules from the list.

4. Remove from the list all rules with no commands.

5. For each pattern rule in the list:

   a. Find the stem s, which is the nonempty part of t or n matched by the '%' in the target pattern.

   b. Compute the dependency names by substituting s for '%'; if the target pattern does not contain a slash, append d to the front of each dependency name.

   c. Test whether all the dependencies exist or ought to exist. (If a file name is mentioned in the makefile as a target or as an explicit dependency, then we say it ought to exist.)

      If all dependencies exist or ought to exist, or there are no dependencies, then this rule applies.

6. If no pattern rule has been found so far, try harder. For each pattern rule in the list:

   a. If the rule is terminal, ignore it and go on to the next rule.

   b. Compute the dependency names as before.

   c. Test whether all the dependencies exist or ought to exist.

   d. For each dependency that does not exist, follow this algorithm recursively to see if the dependency can be made by an implicit rule.

   e. If all dependencies exist, ought to exist, or can be made by implicit rules, then this rule applies.

7. If no implicit rule applies, the rule for .DEFAULT, if any, applies. In that case, give t the same commands that .DEFAULT has. Otherwise, there are no commands for t.

Once a rule that applies has been found, for each target pattern of the rule other than the one that matched t or n, the '%' in the pattern is replaced with s and the resultant file name is stored until the commands to remake the target file t are executed. After these commands are executed, each of these stored file names are entered into the data base and marked as having been updated and having the same update status as the file t.

When the commands of a pattern rule are executed for t, the automatic variables are set corresponding to the target and dependencies. See Section 10.5.3 [Automatic Variables], page 106.

11 Using make to Update Archive Files

Archive files are files containing named subfiles called *members*; they are maintained with the program `ar` and their main use is as subroutine libraries for linking.

11.1 Archive Members as Targets

An individual member of an archive file can be used as a target or dependency in `make`. You specify the member named *member* in archive file *archive* as follows:

    archive(*member*)

This construct is available only in targets and dependencies, not in commands! Most programs that you might use in commands do not support this syntax and cannot act directly on archive members. Only `ar` and other programs specifically designed to operate on archives can do so. Therefore, valid commands to update an archive member target probably must use `ar`. For example, this rule says to create a member 'hack.o' in archive 'foolib' by copying the file 'hack.o':

    foolib(hack.o) : hack.o
            ar cr foolib hack.o

In fact, nearly all archive member targets are updated in just this way and there is an implicit rule to do it for you. **Note:** The 'c' flag to `ar` is required if the archive file does not already exist.

To specify several members in the same archive, you can write all the member names together between the parentheses. For example:

    foolib(hack.o kludge.o)

is equivalent to:

    foolib(hack.o) foolib(kludge.o)

You can also use shell-style wildcards in an archive member reference. See Section 4.2 [Using Wildcard Characters in File Names], page 18. For example, 'foolib(*.o)' expands to all existing members of the 'foolib' archive whose names end in '.o'; perhaps 'foolib(hack.o) foolib(kludge.o)'.

11.2 Implicit Rule for Archive Member Targets

Recall that a target that looks like 'a(m)' stands for the member named m in the archive file a.

When `make` looks for an implicit rule for such a target, as a special feature it considers implicit rules that match '(m)', as well as those that match the actual target 'a(m)'.

This causes one special rule whose target is '(%)' to match. This rule updates the target 'a(m)' by copying the file m into the archive. For example, it will update the archive member target 'foo.a(bar.o)' by copying the file 'bar.o' into the archive 'foo.a' as a member named 'bar.o'.

When this rule is chained with others, the result is very powerful. Thus, 'make "foo.a(bar.o)"' (the quotes are needed to protect the '(' and ')' from being interpreted specially by the shell) in the presence of a file 'bar.c' is enough to cause the following commands to be run, even without a makefile:

```
cc -c bar.c -o bar.o
ar r foo.a bar.o
rm -f bar.o
```

Here make has envisioned the file 'bar.o' as an intermediate file. See Section 10.4 [Chains of Implicit Rules], page 102.

Implicit rules such as this one are written using the automatic variable '$%'. See Section 10.5.3 [Automatic Variables], page 106.

An archive member name in an archive cannot contain a directory name, but it may be useful in a makefile to pretend that it does. If you write an archive member target 'foo.a(dir/file.o)', make will perform automatic updating with this command:

```
ar r foo.a dir/file.o
```

which has the effect of copying the file 'dir/file.o' into a member named 'file.o'. In connection with such usage, the automatic variables %D and %F may be useful.

11.2.1 Updating Archive Symbol Directories

An archive file that is used as a library usually contains a special member named '__.SYMDEF' that contains a directory of the external symbol names defined by all the other members. After you update any other members, you need to update '__.SYMDEF' so that it will summarize the other members properly. This is done by running the `ranlib` program:

```
ranlib archivefile
```

Normally you would put this command in the rule for the archive file, and make all the members of the archive file dependencies of that rule. For example,

```
libfoo.a: libfoo.a(x.o) libfoo.a(y.o) ...
        ranlib libfoo.a
```

The effect of this is to update archive members 'x.o', 'y.o', etc., and then update the symbol directory member '__.SYMDEF' by running `ranlib`. The rules for updating the members are not shown here; most likely you can omit them and use the implicit rule which copies files into the archive, as described in the preceding section.

This is not necessary when using the GNU ar program, which updates the '__.SYMDEF' member automatically.

11.3 Dangers When Using Archives

It is important to be careful when using parallel execution (the -j switch; see Section 5.3 [Parallel Execution], page 39) and archives. If multiple ar commands run at the same time on the same archive file, they will not know about each other and can corrupt the file.

Possibly a future version of make will provide a mechanism to circumvent this problem by serializing all commands that operate on the same archive file. But for the time being, you must either write your makefiles to avoid this problem in some other way, or not use -j.

11.4 Suffix Rules for Archive Files

You can write a special kind of suffix rule for dealing with archive files. See Section 10.7 [Suffix Rules], page 111, for a full explanation of suffix rules. Archive suffix rules are obsolete in GNU make, because pattern rules for archives are a more general mechanism (see Section 11.2 [Archive Update], page 115). But they are retained for compatibility with other makes.

To write a suffix rule for archives, you simply write a suffix rule using the target suffix '.a' (the usual suffix for archive files). For example, here is the old-fashioned suffix rule to update a library archive from C source files:

```
.c.a:
        $(CC) $(CFLAGS) $(CPPFLAGS) -c $< -o $*.o
        $(AR) r $@ $*.o
        $(RM) $*.o
```

This works just as if you had written the pattern rule:

```
(%.o): %.c
        $(CC) $(CFLAGS) $(CPPFLAGS) -c $< -o $*.o
        $(AR) r $@ $*.o
        $(RM) $*.o
```

In fact, this is just what make does when it sees a suffix rule with '.a' as the target suffix. Any double-suffix rule '.x.a' is converted to a pattern rule with the target pattern '(%.o)' and a dependency pattern of '%.x'.

Since you might want to use '.a' as the suffix for some other kind of file, make also converts archive suffix rules to pattern rules in the normal way (see Section 10.7 [Suffix Rules], page 111). Thus a double-suffix rule '.x.a' produces two pattern rules: '(%.o): %.x' and '%.a: %.x'.

12 Features of GNU make

Here is a summary of the features of GNU make, for comparison with and credit to other versions of make. We consider the features of make in 4.2 BSD systems as a baseline. If you are concerned with writing portable makefiles, you should use only the features of make *not* listed here or in Chapter 13 [Missing], page 123.

Many features come from the version of make in System V.

- The VPATH variable and its special meaning. See Section 4.3 [Searching Directories for Dependencies], page 21. This feature exists in System V make, but is undocumented. It is documented in 4.3 BSD make (which says it mimics System V's VPATH feature).

- Included makefiles. See Section 3.3 [Including Other Makefiles], page 12. Allowing multiple files to be included with a single directive is a GNU extension.

- Variables are read from and communicated via the environment. See Section 6.9 [Variables from the Environment], page 62.

- Options passed through the variable MAKEFLAGS to recursive invocations of make. See Section 5.6.3 [Communicating Options to a Sub-make], page 46.

- The automatic variable $% is set to the member name in an archive reference. See Section 10.5.3 [Automatic Variables], page 106.

- The automatic variables $@, $*, $<, $%, and $? have corresponding forms like $(@F) and $(@D). We have generalized this to $^ as an obvious extension. See Section 10.5.3 [Automatic Variables], page 106.

- Substitution variable references. See Section 6.1 [Basics of Variable References], page 51.

- The command-line options '-b' and '-m', accepted and ignored. In System V make, these options actually do something.

- Execution of recursive commands to run make via the variable MAKE even if '-n', '-q' or '-t' is specified. See Section 5.6 [Recursive Use of make], page 42.

- Support for suffix '.a' in suffix rules. See Section 11.4 [Archive Suffix Rules], page 117. This feature is obsolete in GNU make, because the general feature of rule chaining (see Section 10.4 [Chains of Implicit Rules], page 102) allows one pattern rule for installing members in an archive (see Section 11.2 [Archive Update], page 115) to be sufficient.

- The arrangement of lines and backslash-newline combinations in commands is retained when the commands are printed, so they appear as they do in the makefile, except for the stripping of initial whitespace.

The following features were inspired by various other versions of make. In some cases it is unclear exactly which versions inspired which others.

- Pattern rules using '%'. This has been implemented in several versions of make. We're not sure who invented it first, but it's been spread around a bit. See Section 10.5 [Defining and Redefining Pattern Rules], page 103.

- Rule chaining and implicit intermediate files. This was implemented by Stu Feldman in his version of make for AT&T Eighth Edition Research Unix, and later by Andrew Hume of AT&T Bell Labs in his mk program (where he terms it "transitive closure"). We do not really know if we got this from either of them or thought it up ourselves at the same time. See Section 10.4 [Chains of Implicit Rules], page 102.

- The automatic variable $^ containing a list of all dependencies of the current target. We did not invent this, but we have no idea who did. See Section 10.5.3 [Automatic Variables], page 106. The automatic variable $+ is a simple extension of $^.

- The "what if" flag ('-W' in GNU make) was (as far as we know) invented by Andrew Hume in mk. See Section 9.3 [Instead of Executing the Commands], page 85.

- The concept of doing several things at once (parallelism) exists in many incarnations of make and similar programs, though not in the System V or BSD implementations. See Section 5.2 [Command Execution], page 38.

- Modified variable references using pattern substitution come from SunOS 4. See Section 6.1 [Basics of Variable References], page 51. This functionality was provided in GNU make by the patsubst function before the alternate syntax was implemented for compatibility with SunOS 4. It is not altogether clear who inspired whom, since GNU make had patsubst before SunOS 4 was released.

- The special significance of '+' characters preceding command lines (see Section 9.3 [Instead of Executing the Commands], page 85) is mandated by *IEEE Standard 1003.2-1992* (POSIX.2).

- The '+=' syntax to append to the value of a variable comes from SunOS 4 make. See Section 6.6 [Appending More Text to Variables], page 59.

- The syntax '*archive(mem1 mem2...)*' to list multiple members in a single archive file comes from SunOS 4 make. See Section 11.1 [Archive Members], page 115.

- The -include directive to include makefiles with no error for a nonexistent file comes from SunOS 4 make. (But note that SunOS 4 make does not allow multiple makefiles to be specified in one -include directive.) The same feature appears with the name sinclude in SGI make and perhaps others.

The remaining features are inventions new in GNU make:

- Use the '-v' or '--version' option to print version and copyright information.

- Use the '`-h`' or '`--help`' option to summarize the options to `make`.
- Simply-expanded variables. See Section 6.2 [The Two Flavors of Variables], page 52.
- Pass command-line variable assignments automatically through the variable `MAKE` to recursive `make` invocations. See Section 5.6 [Recursive Use of `make`], page 42.
- Use the '`-C`' or '`--directory`' command option to change directory. See Section 9.7 [Summary of Options], page 89.
- Make verbatim variable definitions with `define`. See Section 6.8 [Defining Variables Verbatim], page 61.
- Declare phony targets with the special target `.PHONY`.

  Andrew Hume of AT&T Bell Labs implemented a similar feature with a different syntax in his `mk` program. This seems to be a case of parallel discovery. See Section 4.4 [Phony Targets], page 25.
- Manipulate text by calling functions. See Chapter 8 [Functions for Transforming Text], page 71.
- Use the '`-o`' or '`--old-file`' option to pretend a file's modification-time is old. See Section 9.4 [Avoiding Recompilation of Some Files], page 87.
- Conditional execution.

  This feature has been implemented numerous times in various versions of `make`; it seems a natural extension derived from the features of the C preprocessor and similar macro languages and is not a revolutionary concept. See Chapter 7 [Conditional Parts of Makefiles], page 65.
- Specify a search path for included makefiles. See Section 3.3 [Including Other Makefiles], page 12.
- Specify extra makefiles to read with an environment variable. See Section 3.4 [The Variable `MAKEFILES`], page 13.
- Strip leading sequences of '`./`' from file names, so that '`./`file' and 'file' are considered to be the same file.
- Use a special search method for library dependencies written in the form '`-l`name'. See Section 4.3.6 [Directory Search for Link Libraries], page 25.
- Allow suffixes for suffix rules (see Section 10.7 [Old-Fashioned Suffix Rules], page 111) to contain any characters. In other versions of `make`, they must begin with '`.`' and not contain any '`/`' characters.
- Keep track of the current level of `make` recursion using the variable `MAKELEVEL`. See Section 5.6 [Recursive Use of `make`], page 42.
- Provide any goals given on the command line in the variable `MAKECMDGOALS`. See Section 9.2 [Arguments to Specify the Goals], page 83.

- Specify static pattern rules. See Section 4.10 [Static Pattern Rules], page 31.

- Provide selective `vpath` search. See Section 4.3 [Searching Directories for Dependencies], page 21.

- Provide computed variable references. See Section 6.1 [Basics of Variable References], page 51.

- Update makefiles. See Section 3.5 [How Makefiles Are Remade], page 14. System V `make` has a very, very limited form of this functionality in that it will check out SCCS files for makefiles.

- Various new built-in implicit rules. See Section 10.2 [Catalogue of Implicit Rules], page 96.

- The built-in variable 'MAKE_VERSION' gives the version number of `make`.

13 Incompatibilities and Missing Features

The make programs in various other systems support a few features that are not implemented in GNU make. The POSIX.2 standard (*IEEE Standard 1003.2-1992*) which specifies make does not require any of these features.

- A target of the form '*file*((*entry*))' stands for a member of archive file *file*. The member is chosen, not by name, but by being an object file which defines the linker symbol *entry*.

  This feature was not put into GNU make because of the nonmodularity of putting knowledge into make of the internal format of archive file symbol tables. See Section 11.2.1 [Updating Archive Symbol Directories], page 116.

- Suffixes (used in suffix rules) that end with the character '~' have a special meaning to System V make; they refer to the SCCS file that corresponds to the file one would get without the '~'. For example, the suffix rule '.c~.o' would make the file '*n*.o' from the SCCS file 's.*n*.c'. For complete coverage, a whole series of such suffix rules is required. See Section 10.7 [Old-Fashioned Suffix Rules], page 111.

  In GNU make, this entire series of cases is handled by two pattern rules for extraction from SCCS, in combination with the general feature of rule chaining. See Section 10.4 [Chains of Implicit Rules], page 102.

- In System V make, the string '$$@' has the strange meaning that, in the dependencies of a rule with multiple targets, it stands for the particular target that is being processed.

  This is not defined in GNU make because '$$' should always stand for an ordinary '$'.

  It is possible to get this functionality through the use of static pattern rules (see Section 4.10 [Static Pattern Rules], page 31). The System V make rule:

  ```
  $(targets): $$@.o lib.a
  ```

  can be replaced with the GNU make static pattern rule:

  ```
  $(targets): %: %.o lib.a
  ```

- In System V and 4.3 BSD make, files found by VPATH search (see Section 4.3 [Searching Directories for Dependencies], page 21) have their names changed inside command strings. We feel it is much cleaner to always use automatic variables and thus make this feature obsolete.

- In some Unix makes, the automatic variable $* appearing in the dependencies of a rule has the amazingly strange "feature" of expanding to the full name of the *target of that rule*. We cannot imagine what went on in the minds of Unix make developers to do this; it is utterly inconsistent with the normal definition of $*.

- In some Unix `make`s, implicit rule search (see Chapter 10 [Using Implicit Rules], page 95) is apparently done for *all* targets, not just those without commands. This means you can do:

  ```
  foo.o:
          cc -c foo.c
  ```

  and Unix `make` will intuit that 'foo.o' depends on 'foo.c'.

  We feel that such usage is broken. The dependency properties of `make` are well-defined (for GNU `make`, at least), and doing such a thing simply does not fit the model.

- GNU `make` does not include any built-in implicit rules for compiling or preprocessing EFL programs. If we hear of anyone who is using EFL, we will gladly add them.

- It appears that in SVR4 `make`, a suffix rule can be specified with no commands, and it is treated as if it had empty commands (see Section 5.8 [Empty Commands], page 49). For example:

  ```
  .c.a:
  ```

  will override the built-in '.c.a' suffix rule.

  We feel that it is cleaner for a rule without commands to always simply add to the dependency list for the target. The above example can be easily rewritten to get the desired behavior in GNU `make`:

  ```
  .c.a: ;
  ```

- Some versions of `make` invoke the shell with the '-e' flag, except under '-k' (see Section 9.6 [Testing the Compilation of a Program], page 88). The '-e' flag tells the shell to exit as soon as any program it runs returns a nonzero status. We feel it is cleaner to write each shell command line to stand on its own and not require this special treatment.

14 Makefile Conventions

This chapter describes conventions for writing the Makefiles for GNU programs.

14.1 General Conventions for Makefiles

Every Makefile should contain this line:

```
SHELL = /bin/sh
```

to avoid trouble on systems where the SHELL variable might be inherited from the environment. (This is never a problem with GNU make.)

Different make programs have incompatible suffix lists and implicit rules, and this sometimes creates confusion or misbehavior. So it is a good idea to set the suffix list explicitly using only the suffixes you need in the particular Makefile, like this:

```
.SUFFIXES:
.SUFFIXES: .c .o
```

The first line clears out the suffix list, the second introduces all suffixes which may be subject to implicit rules in this Makefile.

Don't assume that '.' is in the path for command execution. When you need to run programs that are a part of your package during the make, please make sure that it uses './' if the program is built as part of the make or '$(srcdir)/' if the file is an unchanging part of the source code. Without one of these prefixes, the current search path is used.

The distinction between './' (the *build directory*) and '$(srcdir)/' (the *source directory*) is important because users can build in a separate directory using the '--srcdir' option to 'configure'. A rule of the form:

```
foo.1 : foo.man sedscript
        sed -e sedscript foo.man > foo.1
```

will fail when the build directory is not the source directory, because 'foo.man' and 'sedscript' are in the the source directory.

When using GNU make, relying on 'VPATH' to find the source file will work in the case where there is a single dependency file, since the make automatic variable '$<' will represent the source file wherever it is. (Many versions of make set '$<' only in implicit rules.) A Makefile target like

```
foo.o : bar.c
        $(CC) -I. -I$(srcdir) $(CFLAGS) -c bar.c -o foo.o
```

should instead be written as

```
foo.o : bar.c
        $(CC) -I. -I$(srcdir) $(CFLAGS) -c $< -o $@
```

in order to allow 'VPATH' to work correctly. When the target has multiple dependencies, using an explicit '$(srcdir)' is the easiest way to make the rule work well. For example, the target above for 'foo.1' is best written as:

```
foo.1 : foo.man sedscript
        sed -e $(srcdir)/sedscript $(srcdir)/foo.man > $@
```

GNU distributions usually contain some files which are not source files—for example, Info files, and the output from Autoconf, Automake, Bison or Flex. Since these files normally appear in the source directory, they should always appear in the source directory, not in the build directory. So Makefile rules to update them should put the updated files in the source directory.

However, if a file does not appear in the distribution, then the Makefile should not put it in the source directory, because building a program in ordinary circumstances should not modify the source directory in any way.

Try to make the build and installation targets, at least (and all their subtargets) work correctly with a parallel `make`.

14.2 Utilities in Makefiles

Write the Makefile commands (and any shell scripts, such as `configure`) to run in `sh`, not in `csh`. Don't use any special features of `ksh` or `bash`.

The `configure` script and the Makefile rules for building and installation should not use any utilities directly except these:

```
cat cmp cp diff echo egrep expr false grep install-info
ln ls mkdir mv pwd rm rmdir sed sleep sort tar test touch true
```

The compression program `gzip` can be used in the `dist` rule.

Stick to the generally supported options for these programs. For example, don't use 'mkdir -p', convenient as it may be, because most systems don't support it.

It is a good idea to avoid creating symbolic links in makefiles, since a few systems don't support them.

The Makefile rules for building and installation can also use compilers and related programs, but should do so via `make` variables so that the user can substitute alternatives. Here are some of the programs we mean:

```
ar bison cc flex install ld ldconfig lex
make makeinfo ranlib texi2dvi yacc
```

Use the following `make` variables to run those programs:

```
$(AR) $(BISON) $(CC) $(FLEX) $(INSTALL) $(LD) $(LDCONFIG) $(LEX)
$(MAKE) $(MAKEINFO) $(RANLIB) $(TEXI2DVI) $(YACC)
```

When you use `ranlib` or `ldconfig`, you should make sure nothing bad happens if the system does not have the program in question. Arrange to ignore an error from that command, and print a message before the command to tell the user that failure of this command does not mean a problem. (The Autoconf 'AC_PROG_RANLIB' macro can help with this.)

If you use symbolic links, you should implement a fallback for systems that don't have symbolic links.

Additional utilities that can be used via Make variables are:

```
chgrp chmod chown mknod
```

It is ok to use other utilities in Makefile portions (or scripts) intended only for particular systems where you know those utilities exist.

14.3 Variables for Specifying Commands

Makefiles should provide variables for overriding certain commands, options, and so on.

In particular, you should run most utility programs via variables. Thus, if you use Bison, have a variable named BISON whose default value is set with 'BISON = bison', and refer to it with $(BISON) whenever you need to use Bison.

File management utilities such as ln, rm, mv, and so on, need not be referred to through variables in this way, since users don't need to replace them with other programs.

Each program-name variable should come with an options variable that is used to supply options to the program. Append 'FLAGS' to the program-name variable name to get the options variable name—for example, BISONFLAGS. (The names CFLAGS for the C compiler, YFLAGS for yacc, and LFLAGS for lex, are exceptions to this rule, but we keep them because they are standard.) Use CPPFLAGS in any compilation command that runs the preprocessor, and use LDFLAGS in any compilation command that does linking as well as in any direct use of ld.

If there are C compiler options that *must* be used for proper compilation of certain files, do not include them in CFLAGS. Users expect to be able to specify CFLAGS freely themselves. Instead, arrange to pass the necessary options to the C compiler independently of CFLAGS, by writing them explicitly in the compilation commands or by defining an implicit rule, like this:

```
CFLAGS = -g
ALL_CFLAGS = -I. $(CFLAGS)
.c.o:
        $(CC) -c $(CPPFLAGS) $(ALL_CFLAGS) $<
```

Do include the '-g' option in CFLAGS, because that is not *required* for proper compilation. You can consider it a default that is only recommended. If the package is set up so that it is compiled with GCC by default, then you might as well include '-O' in the default value of CFLAGS as well.

Put CFLAGS last in the compilation command, after other variables containing compiler options, so the user can use CFLAGS to override the others.

CFLAGS should be used in every invocation of the C compiler, both those which do compilation and those which do linking.

Every Makefile should define the variable INSTALL, which is the basic command for installing a file into the system.

Every Makefile should also define the variables INSTALL_PROGRAM and INSTALL_DATA. (The default for each of these should be $(INSTALL).) Then it should use those variables as the commands for actual installation, for executables and nonexecutables respectively. Use these variables as follows:

```
$(INSTALL_PROGRAM) foo $(bindir)/foo
$(INSTALL_DATA) libfoo.a $(libdir)/libfoo.a
```

Always use a file name, not a directory name, as the second argument of the installation commands. Use a separate command for each file to be installed.

14.4 Variables for Installation Directories

Installation directories should always be named by variables, so it is easy to install in a nonstandard place. The standard names for these variables are described below. They are based on a standard filesystem layout; variants of it are used in SVR4, 4.4BSD, Linux, Ultrix v4, and other modern operating systems.

These two variables set the root for the installation. All the other installation directories should be subdirectories of one of these two, and nothing should be directly installed into these two directories.

'prefix'   A prefix used in constructing the default values of the variables listed below. The default value of prefix should be '/usr/local'. When building the complete GNU system, the prefix will be empty and '/usr' will be a symbolic link to '/'. (If you are using Autoconf, write it as '@prefix@'.)

'exec_prefix'
              A prefix used in constructing the default values of some of the variables listed below. The default value of exec_prefix should be $(prefix). (If you are using Autoconf, write it as '@exec_prefix@'.)

              Generally, $(exec_prefix) is used for directories that contain machine-specific files (such as executables and subroutine libraries), while $(prefix) is used directly for other directories.

Executable programs are installed in one of the following directories.

'bindir'   The directory for installing executable programs that users can run. This should normally be '/usr/local/bin', but write it as

'$(exec_prefix)/bin'. (If you are using Autoconf, write it as
'@bindir@'.)

'sbindir'   The directory for installing executable programs that can be run
            from the shell, but are only generally useful to system adminis-
            trators. This should normally be '/usr/local/sbin', but write
            it as '$(exec_prefix)/sbin'. (If you are using Autoconf, write
            it as '@sbindir@'.)

'libexecdir'
            The directory for installing executable programs to be run
            by other programs rather than by users. This directory
            should normally be '/usr/local/libexec', but write it as
            '$(exec_prefix)/libexec'. (If you are using Autoconf, write
            it as '@libexecdir@'.)

Data files used by the program during its execution are divided into
categories in two ways.

- Some files are normally modified by programs; others are never normally
  modified (though users may edit some of these).
- Some files are architecture-independent and can be shared by all machines at a site; some are architecture-dependent and can be shared only
  by machines of the same kind and operating system; others may never
  be shared between two machines.

This makes for six different possibilities. However, we want to discourage
the use of architecture-dependent files, aside from object files and libraries.
It is much cleaner to make other data files architecture-independent, and it
is generally not hard.

Therefore, here are the variables Makefiles should use to specify directories:

'datadir'   The directory for installing read-only architecture independent
            data files. This should normally be '/usr/local/share', but
            write it as '$(prefix)/share'. (If you are using Autoconf, write
            it as '@datadir@'.) As a special exception, see '$(infodir)' and
            '$(includedir)' below.

'sysconfdir'
            The directory for installing read-only data files that pertain to a
            single machine–that is to say, files for configuring a host. Mailer
            and network configuration files, '/etc/passwd', and so forth be-
            long here. All the files in this directory should be ordinary ASCII
            text files. This directory should normally be '/usr/local/etc',
            but write it as '$(prefix)/etc'. (If you are using Autoconf,
            write it as '@sysconfdir@'.)

            Do not install executables here in this directory (they probably
            belong in '$(libexecdir)' or '$(sbindir)'). Also do not install

files that are modified in the normal course of their use (programs whose purpose is to change the configuration of the system excluded). Those probably belong in '$(localstatedir)'.

'sharedstatedir'
> The directory for installing architecture-independent data files which the programs modify while they run. This should normally be '/usr/local/com', but write it as '$(prefix)/com'. (If you are using Autoconf, write it as '@sharedstatedir@'.)

'localstatedir'
> The directory for installing data files which the programs modify while they run, and that pertain to one specific machine. Users should never need to modify files in this directory to configure the package's operation; put such configuration information in separate files that go in '$(datadir)' or '$(sysconfdir)'. '$(localstatedir)' should normally be '/usr/local/var', but write it as '$(prefix)/var'. (If you are using Autoconf, write it as '@localstatedir@'.)

'libdir'   The directory for object files and libraries of object code. Do not install executables here, they probably ought to go in '$(libexecdir)' instead. The value of libdir should normally be '/usr/local/lib', but write it as '$(exec_prefix)/lib'. (If you are using Autoconf, write it as '@libdir@'.)

'infodir'   The directory for installing the Info files for this package. By default, it should be '/usr/local/info', but it should be written as '$(prefix)/info'. (If you are using Autoconf, write it as '@infodir@'.)

'lispdir'   The directory for installing any Emacs Lisp files in this package. By default, it should be '/usr/local/share/emacs/site-lisp', but it should be written as '$(prefix)/share/emacs/site-lisp'.

> If you are using Autoconf, write the default as '@lispdir@'. In order to make '@lispdir@' work, you need the following lines in your 'configure.in' file:

```
lispdir='${datadir}/emacs/site-lisp'
AC_SUBST(lispdir)
```

'includedir'
> The directory for installing header files to be included by user programs with the C '#include' preprocessor directive. This should normally be '/usr/local/include', but write it as '$(prefix)/include'. (If you are using Autoconf, write it as '@includedir@'.)

> Most compilers other than GCC do not look for header files in directory '/usr/local/include'. So installing the header files

this way is only useful with GCC. Sometimes this is not a problem because some libraries are only really intended to work with GCC. But some libraries are intended to work with other compilers. They should install their header files in two places, one specified by `includedir` and one specified by `oldincludedir`.

'oldincludedir'
> The directory for installing '#include' header files for use with compilers other than GCC. This should normally be '/usr/include'. (If you are using Autoconf, you can write it as '@oldincludedir@'.)
>
> The Makefile commands should check whether the value of `oldincludedir` is empty. If it is, they should not try to use it; they should cancel the second installation of the header files.
>
> A package should not replace an existing header in this directory unless the header came from the same package. Thus, if your Foo package provides a header file 'foo.h', then it should install the header file in the `oldincludedir` directory if either (1) there is no 'foo.h' there or (2) the 'foo.h' that exists came from the Foo package.
>
> To tell whether 'foo.h' came from the Foo package, put a magic string in the file—part of a comment—and `grep` for that string.

Unix-style man pages are installed in one of the following:

'mandir'
> The top-level directory for installing the man pages (if any) for this package. It will normally be '/usr/local/man', but you should write it as '$(prefix)/man'. (If you are using Autoconf, write it as '@mandir@'.)

'man1dir'
> The directory for installing section 1 man pages. Write it as '$(mandir)/man1'.

'man2dir'
> The directory for installing section 2 man pages. Write it as '$(mandir)/man2'

'...'
> **Don't make the primary documentation for any GNU software be a man page. Write a manual in Texinfo instead. Man pages are just for the sake of people running GNU software on Unix, which is a secondary application only.**

'manext'
> The file name extension for the installed man page. This should contain a period followed by the appropriate digit; it should normally be '.1'.

'man1ext'
> The file name extension for installed section 1 man pages.

'man2ext'
> The file name extension for installed section 2 man pages.

'...'   Use these names instead of 'manext' if the package needs to
             install man pages in more than one section of the manual.

And finally, you should set the following variable:

'srcdir'   The directory for the sources being compiled. The value of this
             variable is normally inserted by the configure shell script. (If
             you are using Autconf, use 'srcdir = @srcdir@'.)

For example:

```
# Common prefix for installation directories.
# NOTE: This directory must exist when you start the install.
prefix = /usr/local
exec_prefix = $(prefix)
# Where to put the executable for the command 'gcc'.
bindir = $(exec_prefix)/bin
# Where to put the directories used by the compiler.
libexecdir = $(exec_prefix)/libexec
# Where to put the Info files.
infodir = $(prefix)/info
```

If your program installs a large number of files into one of the standard
user-specified directories, it might be useful to group them into a subdirectory particular to that program. If you do this, you should write the install
rule to create these subdirectories.

Do not expect the user to include the subdirectory name in the value
of any of the variables listed above. The idea of having a uniform set of
variable names for installation directories is to enable the user to specify the
exact same values for several different GNU packages. In order for this to
be useful, all the packages must be designed so that they will work sensibly
when the user does so.

14.5 Standard Targets for Users

All GNU programs should have the following targets in their Makefiles:

'all'   Compile the entire program. This should be the default target.
             This target need not rebuild any documentation files; Info files
             should normally be included in the distribution, and DVI files
             should be made only when explicitly asked for.

             By default, the Make rules should compile and link with '-g', so
             that executable programs have debugging symbols. Users who
             don't mind being helpless can strip the executables later if they
             wish.

'install'   Compile the program and copy the executables, libraries, and
             so on to the file names where they should reside for actual use.

If there is a simple test to verify that a program is properly installed, this target should run that test.

Do not strip executables when installing them. Devil-may-care users can use the install-strip target to do that.

If possible, write the install target rule so that it does not modify anything in the directory where the program was built, provided 'make all' has just been done. This is convenient for building the program under one user name and installing it under another.

The commands should create all the directories in which files are to be installed, if they don't already exist. This includes the directories specified as the values of the variables prefix and exec_prefix, as well as all subdirectories that are needed. One way to do this is by means of an installdirs target as described below.

Use '-' before any command for installing a man page, so that make will ignore any errors. This is in case there are systems that don't have the Unix man page documentation system installed.

The way to install Info files is to copy them into '$(infodir)' with $(INSTALL_DATA) (see Section 14.3 [Command Variables], page 127), and then run the install-info program if it is present. install-info is a program that edits the Info 'dir' file to add or update the menu entry for the given Info file; it is part of the Texinfo package. Here is a sample rule to install an Info file:

```
$(infodir)/foo.info: foo.info
        $(POST_INSTALL)
# There may be a newer info file in . than in srcdir.
        -if test -f foo.info; then d=.; \
        else d=$(srcdir); fi; \
        $(INSTALL_DATA) $$d/foo.info $@; \
# Run install-info only if it exists.
# Use 'if' instead of just prepending '-' to the
# line so we notice real errors from install-info.
# We use '$(SHELL) -c' because some shells do not
# fail gracefully when there is an unknown command.
        if $(SHELL) -c 'install-info --version' \
           >/dev/null 2>&1; then \
          install-info --dir-file=$(infodir)/dir \
                       $(infodir)/foo.info; \
        else true; fi
```

When writing the install target, you must classify all the commands into three categories: normal ones, *pre-installation* commands and *post-installation* commands. See Section 14.6 [Install Command Categories], page 137.

'uninstall'

> Delete all the installed files—the copies that the 'install' target creates.
>
> This rule should not modify the directories where compilation is done, only the directories where files are installed.
>
> The uninstallation commands are divided into three categories, just like the installation commands. See Section 14.6 [Install Command Categories], page 137.

'install-strip'

> Like install, but strip the executable files while installing them. In many cases, the definition of this target can be very simple:
>
> ```
> install-strip:
>         $(MAKE) INSTALL_PROGRAM='$(INSTALL_PROGRAM) -s' \
>                 install
> ```
>
> Normally we do not recommend stripping an executable unless you are sure the program has no bugs. However, it can be reasonable to install a stripped executable for actual execution while saving the unstripped executable elsewhere in case there is a bug.

'clean'

> Delete all files from the current directory that are normally created by building the program. Don't delete the files that record the configuration. Also preserve files that could be made by building, but normally aren't because the distribution comes with them.
>
> Delete '.dvi' files here if they are not part of the distribution.

'distclean'

> Delete all files from the current directory that are created by configuring or building the program. If you have unpacked the source and built the program without creating any other files, 'make distclean' should leave only the files that were in the distribution.

'mostlyclean'

> Like 'clean', but may refrain from deleting a few files that people normally don't want to recompile. For example, the 'mostlyclean' target for GCC does not delete 'libgcc.a', because recompiling it is rarely necessary and takes a lot of time.

'maintainer-clean'

> Delete almost everything from the current directory that can be reconstructed with this Makefile. This typically includes everything deleted by `distclean`, plus more: C source files produced by Bison, tags tables, Info files, and so on.
>
> The reason we say "almost everything" is that running the command 'make maintainer-clean' should not delete 'configure' even if 'configure' can be remade using a rule in the Makefile. More generally, 'make maintainer-clean' should not delete anything that needs to exist in order to run 'configure' and then begin to build the program. This is the only exception; maintainer-clean should delete everything else that can be rebuilt.
>
> The 'maintainer-clean' target is intended to be used by a maintainer of the package, not by ordinary users. You may need special tools to reconstruct some of the files that 'make maintainer-clean' deletes. Since these files are normally included in the distribution, we don't take care to make them easy to reconstruct. If you find you need to unpack the full distribution again, don't blame us.
>
> To help make users aware of this, the commands for the special maintainer-clean target should start with these two:
>
> ```
> @echo 'This command is intended for maintainers to use; it'
> @echo 'deletes files that may need special tools to rebuild.'
> ```

'TAGS'   Update a tags table for this program.

'info'   Generate any Info files needed. The best way to write the rules is as follows:

> ```
> info: foo.info
>
>
> foo.info: foo.texi chap1.texi chap2.texi
>         $(MAKEINFO) $(srcdir)/foo.texi
> ```
>
> You must define the variable MAKEINFO in the Makefile. It should run the makeinfo program, which is part of the Texinfo distribution.
>
> Normally a GNU distribution comes with Info files, and that means the Info files are present in the source directory. Therefore, the Make rule for an info file should update it in the source directory. When users build the package, ordinarily Make will not update the Info files because they will already be up to date.

'dvi'   Generate DVI files for all Texinfo documentation. For example:

> ```
> dvi: foo.dvi
> ```

```
foo.dvi: foo.texi chap1.texi chap2.texi
        $(TEXI2DVI) $(srcdir)/foo.texi
```

You must define the variable TEXI2DVI in the Makefile. It should run the program texi2dvi, which is part of the Texinfo distribution.[1] Alternatively, write just the dependencies, and allow GNU make to provide the command.

'dist'   Create a distribution tar file for this program. The tar file should be set up so that the file names in the tar file start with a subdirectory name which is the name of the package it is a distribution for. This name can include the version number.

For example, the distribution tar file of GCC version 1.40 unpacks into a subdirectory named 'gcc-1.40'.

The easiest way to do this is to create a subdirectory appropriately named, use ln or cp to install the proper files in it, and then tar that subdirectory.

Compress the tar file file with gzip. For example, the actual distribution file for GCC version 1.40 is called 'gcc-1.40.tar.gz'.

The dist target should explicitly depend on all non-source files that are in the distribution, to make sure they are up to date in the distribution. See section "Making Releases" in *GNU Coding Standards*.

'check'   Perform self-tests (if any). The user must build the program before running the tests, but need not install the program; you should write the self-tests so that they work when the program is built but not installed.

The following targets are suggested as conventional names, for programs in which they are useful.

installcheck
           Perform installation tests (if any). The user must build and install the program before running the tests. You should not assume that '$(bindir)' is in the search path.

installdirs
           It's useful to add a target named 'installdirs' to create the directories where files are installed, and their parent directories. There is a script called 'mkinstalldirs' which is convenient for this; you can find it in the Texinfo package. You can use a rule like this:

---

[1] texi2dvi uses TeX to do the real work of formatting. TeX is not distributed with Texinfo.

```
# Make sure all installation directories (e.g. $(bindir))
# actually exist by making them if necessary.
installdirs: mkinstalldirs
        $(srcdir)/mkinstalldirs $(bindir) $(datadir) \
                                $(libdir) $(infodir) \
                                $(mandir)
```

This rule should not modify the directories where compilation is done. It should do nothing but create installation directories.

14.6 Install Command Categories

When writing the install target, you must classify all the commands into three categories: normal ones, *pre-installation* commands and *post-installation* commands.

Normal commands move files into their proper places, and set their modes. They may not alter any files except the ones that come entirely from the package they belong to.

Pre-installation and post-installation commands may alter other files; in particular, they can edit global configuration files or data bases.

Pre-installation commands are typically executed before the normal commands, and post-installation commands are typically run after the normal commands.

The most common use for a post-installation command is to run install-info. This cannot be done with a normal command, since it alters a file (the Info directory) which does not come entirely and solely from the package being installed. It is a post-installation command because it needs to be done after the normal command which installs the package's Info files.

Most programs don't need any pre-installation commands, but we have the feature just in case it is needed.

To classify the commands in the install rule into these three categories, insert *category lines* among them. A category line specifies the category for the commands that follow.

A category line consists of a tab and a reference to a special Make variable, plus an optional comment at the end. There are three variables you can use, one for each category; the variable name specifies the category. Category lines are no-ops in ordinary execution because these three Make variables are normally undefined (and you *should not* define them in the makefile).

Here are the three possible category lines, each with a comment that explains what it means:

```
$(PRE_INSTALL)      # Pre-install commands follow.
$(POST_INSTALL)     # Post-install commands follow.
$(NORMAL_INSTALL)   # Normal commands follow.
```

If you don't use a category line at the beginning of the `install` rule, all
the commands are classified as normal until the first category line. If you
don't use any category lines, all the commands are classified as normal.

These are the category lines for `uninstall`:

```
$(PRE_UNINSTALL)      # Pre-uninstall commands follow.
$(POST_UNINSTALL)     # Post-uninstall commands follow.
$(NORMAL_UNINSTALL)   # Normal commands follow.
```

Typically, a pre-uninstall command would be used for deleting entries
from the Info directory.

If the `install` or `uninstall` target has any dependencies which act as
subroutines of installation, then you should start *each* dependency's commands with a category line, and start the main target's commands with a
category line also. This way, you can ensure that each command is placed
in the right category regardless of which of the dependencies actually run.

Pre-installation and post-installation commands should not run any programs except for these:

```
[ basename bash cat chgrp chmod chown cmp cp dd diff echo
egrep expand expr false fgrep find getopt grep gunzip gzip
hostname install install-info kill ldconfig ln ls md5sum
mkdir mkfifo mknod mv printenv pwd rm rmdir sed sort tee
test touch true uname xargs yes
```

The reason for distinguishing the commands in this way is for the sake of
making binary packages. Typically a binary package contains all the executables and other files that need to be installed, and has its own method of installing them—so it does not need to run the normal installation commands.
But installing the binary package does need to execute the pre-installation
and post-installation commands.

Programs to build binary packages work by extracting the pre-installation
and post-installation commands. Here is one way of extracting the pre-
installation commands:

```
make -n install -o all \
      PRE_INSTALL=pre-install \
      POST_INSTALL=post-install \
      NORMAL_INSTALL=normal-install \
   | gawk -f pre-install.awk
```

where the file 'pre-install.awk' could contain this:

```
$0 ~ /^\t[ \t]*(normal_install|post_install)[ \t]*$/ {on = 0}
on {print $0}
$0 ~ /^\t[ \t]*pre_install[ \t]*$/ {on = 1}
```

The resulting file of pre-installation commands is executed as a shell script
as part of installing the binary package.

Appendix A Quick Reference

This appendix summarizes the directives, text manipulation functions, and special variables which GNU `make` understands. See Section 4.7 [Special Targets], page 28, Section 10.2 [Catalogue of Implicit Rules], page 96, and Section 9.7 [Summary of Options], page 89, for other summaries.

Here is a summary of the directives GNU `make` recognizes:

`define` *variable*
`endef`

> Define a multi-line, recursively-expanded variable.
> See Section 5.7 [Sequences], page 48.

`ifdef` *variable*
`ifndef` *variable*
`ifeq` (a,b)
`ifeq "a" "b"`
`ifeq 'a' 'b'`
`ifneq` (a,b)
`ifneq "a" "b"`
`ifneq 'a' 'b'`
`else`
`endif`

> Conditionally evaluate part of the makefile.
> See Chapter 7 [Conditionals], page 65.

`include` *file*

> Include another makefile.
> See Section 3.3 [Including Other Makefiles], page 12.

`override` *variable* = *value*
`override` *variable* := *value*
`override` *variable* += *value*
`override` `define` *variable*
`endef`

> Define a variable, overriding any previous definition, even one from the command line.
> See Section 6.7 [The `override` Directive], page 61.

`export`

> Tell `make` to export all variables to child processes by default.
> See Section 5.6.2 [Communicating Variables to a Sub-`make`], page 44.

`export` *variable*
`export` *variable* = *value*
`export` *variable* := *value*
`export` *variable* += *value*
`unexport` *variable*

> Tell `make` whether or not to export a particular variable to child processes.
> See Section 5.6.2 [Communicating Variables to a Sub-make], page 44.

`vpath` *pattern path*

> Specify a search path for files matching a '%' pattern.
> See Section 4.3.2 [The `vpath` Directive], page 21.

`vpath` *pattern*

> Remove all search paths previously specified for *pattern*.

`vpath`

> Remove all search paths previously specified in any `vpath` directive.

Here is a summary of the text manipulation functions (see Chapter 8 [Functions], page 71):

`$(subst` *from*, *to*, *text*`)`

> Replace *from* with *to* in *text*.
> See Section 8.2 [Functions for String Substitution and Analysis], page 72.

`$(patsubst` *pattern*, *replacement*, *text*`)`

> Replace words matching *pattern* with *replacement* in *text*.
> See Section 8.2 [Functions for String Substitution and Analysis], page 72.

`$(strip` *string*`)`

> Remove excess whitespace characters from *string*.
> See Section 8.2 [Functions for String Substitution and Analysis], page 72.

`$(findstring` *find*, *text*`)`

> Locate *find* in *text*.
> See Section 8.2 [Functions for String Substitution and Analysis], page 72.

`$(filter` *pattern*..., *text*`)`

> Select words in *text* that match one of the *pattern* words.
> See Section 8.2 [Functions for String Substitution and Analysis], page 72.

$(filter-out *pattern...*, *text*)

> Select words in *text* that *do not* match any of the *pattern* words.
> See Section 8.2 [Functions for String Substitution and Analysis],
> page 72.

$(sort *list*)

> Sort the words in *list* lexicographically, removing duplicates.
> See Section 8.2 [Functions for String Substitution and Analysis],
> page 72.

$(dir *names...*)

> Extract the directory part of each file name.
> See Section 8.3 [Functions for File Names], page 75.

$(notdir *names...*)

> Extract the non-directory part of each file name.
> See Section 8.3 [Functions for File Names], page 75.

$(suffix *names...*)

> Extract the suffix (the last '.' and following characters) of each
> file name.
> See Section 8.3 [Functions for File Names], page 75.

$(basename *names...*)

> Extract the base name (name without suffix) of each file name.
> See Section 8.3 [Functions for File Names], page 75.

$(addsuffix *suffix*, *names...*)

> Append *suffix* to each word in *names*.
> See Section 8.3 [Functions for File Names], page 75.

$(addprefix *prefix*, *names...*)

> Prepend *prefix* to each word in *names*.
> See Section 8.3 [Functions for File Names], page 75.

$(join *list1*, *list2*)

> Join two parallel lists of words.
> See Section 8.3 [Functions for File Names], page 75.

$(word *n*, *text*)

> Extract the *n*th word (one-origin) of *text*.
> See Section 8.3 [Functions for File Names], page 75.

$(words *text*)

> Count the number of words in *text*.
> See Section 8.3 [Functions for File Names], page 75.

$(firstword *names...*)

> Extract the first word of *names*.
> See Section 8.3 [Functions for File Names], page 75.

$(wildcard *pattern...*)
    Find file names matching a shell file name pattern (*not a* '%' pattern).
    See Section 4.2.3 [The Function wildcard], page 20.

$(shell *command*)
    Execute a shell command and return its output.
    See Section 8.6 [The shell Function], page 81.

$(origin *variable*)
    Return a string describing how the make variable *variable* was defined.
    See Section 8.5 [The origin Function], page 79.

$(foreach *var*, *words*, *text*)
    Evaluate *text* with *var* bound to each word in *words*, and concatenate the results.
    See Section 8.4 [The foreach Function], page 78.

Here is a summary of the automatic variables. See Section 10.5.3 [Automatic Variables], page 106, for full information.

$@   The file name of the target.

$%   The target member name, when the target is an archive member.

$<   The name of the first dependency.

$?   The names of all the dependencies that are newer than the target, with spaces between them. For dependencies which are archive members, only the member named is used (see Chapter 11 [Archives], page 115).

$^

$+   The names of all the dependencies, with spaces between them. For dependencies which are archive members, only the member named is used (see Chapter 11 [Archives], page 115). The value of $^ omits duplicate dependencies, while $+ retains them and preserves their order.

$*   The stem with which an implicit rule matches (see Section 10.5.4 [How Patterns Match], page 108).

$(@D)

$(@F)   The directory part and the file-within-directory part of $@.

$(*D)

$(*F)   The directory part and the file-within-directory part of $*.

$(%D)

$(%F)   The directory part and the file-within-directory part of $%.

`$(<D)`
`$(<F)`   The directory part and the file-within-directory part of `$<`.

`$(^D)`
`$(^F)`   The directory part and the file-within-directory part of `$^`.

`$(+D)`
`$(+F)`   The directory part and the file-within-directory part of `$+`.

`$(?D)`
`$(?F)`   The directory part and the file-within-directory part of `$?`.

These variables are used specially by GNU `make`:

MAKEFILES
        Makefiles to be read on every invocation of `make`.
        See Section 3.4 [The Variable `MAKEFILES`], page 13.

VPATH
        Directory search path for files not found in the current directory.
        See Section 4.3.1 [`VPATH` Search Path for All Dependencies],
        page 21.

SHELL
        The name of the system default command interpreter, usually
        '/bin/sh'. You can set `SHELL` in the makefile to change the shell
        used to run commands. See Section 5.2 [Command Execution],
        page 38.

MAKESHELL
        On MS-DOS only, the name of the command interpreter that is
        to be used by `make`. This value takes precedence over the value
        of `SHELL`. See Section 5.2 [MAKESHELL variable], page 38.

MAKE
        The name with which `make` was invoked. Using this variable
        in commands has special meaning. See Section 5.6.1 [How the
        `MAKE` Variable Works], page 43.

MAKELEVEL
        The number of levels of recursion (sub-`make`s).
        See Section 5.6.2 [Variables/Recursion], page 44.

MAKEFLAGS
        The flags given to `make`. You can set this in the environment or
        a makefile to set flags.
        See Section 5.6.3 [Communicating Options to a Sub-`make`],
        page 46.

MAKECMDGOALS

> The targets given to make on the command line. Setting this variable has no effect on the operation of make.
> See Section 9.2 [Arguments to Specify the Goals], page 83.

CURDIR

> Set to the pathname of the current working directory (after all -C options are processed, if any). Setting this variable has no effect on the operation of make.
> See Section 5.6 [Recursive Use of make], page 42.

SUFFIXES

> The default list of suffixes before make reads any makefiles.

Appendix B Errors Generated by Make

Here is a list of the most common errors you might see generated by make, and some information about what they mean and how to fix them.

Sometimes make errors are not fatal, especially in the presence of a - prefix on a command script line, or the -k command line option. Errors that are fatal are prefixed with the string ***.

Error messages are all either prefixed with the name of the program (usually 'make'), or, if the error is found in a makefile, the name of the file and linenumber containing the problem.

In the table below, these common prefixes are left off.

'[*foo*] Error *NN*'
'[*foo*] *signal description*'

> These errors are not really make errors at all. They mean that a program that make invoked as part of a command script returned a non-0 error code ('Error *NN*'), which make interprets as failure, or it exited in some other abnormal fashion (with a signal of some type).
>
> If no *** is attached to the message, then the subprocess failed but the rule in the makefile was prefixed with the - special character, so make ignored the error.

'missing separator. Stop.'

> This is make's generic "Huh?" error message. It means that make was completely unsuccessful at parsing this line of your makefile. It basically means "syntax error".
>
> One of the most common reasons for this message is that you (or perhaps your oh-so-helpful editor, as is the case with many MS-Windows editors) have attempted to indent your command scripts with spaces instead of a TAB character. Remember that every line in the command script must begin with a TAB character. Eight spaces do not count.

'commands commence before first target. Stop.'
'missing rule before commands. Stop.'

> This means the first thing in the makefile seems to be part of a command script: it begins with a TAB character and doesn't appear to be a legal make command (such as a variable assignment). Command scripts must always be associated with a target.
>
> The second form is generated if the line has a semicolon as the first non-whitespace character; make interprets this to mean you left out the "target: dependency" section of a rule.

'No rule to make target 'xxx'.'
'No rule to make target 'xxx', needed by 'yyy'.'
> This means that make decided it needed to build a target, but then couldn't find any instructions in the makefile on how to do that, either explicit or implicit (including in the default rules database).

> If you want that file to be built, you will need to add a rule to your makefile describing how that target can be built. Other possible sources of this problem are typos in the makefile (if that filename is wrong) or a corrupted source tree (if that file is not supposed to be built, but rather only a dependency).

'No targets specified and no makefile found. Stop.'
'No targets. Stop.'
> The former means that you didn't provide any targets to be built on the command line, and make couldn't find any makefiles to read in. The latter means that some makefile was found, but it didn't contain any default target and none was given on the command line. GNU make has nothing to do in these situations.

'Makefile 'xxx' was not found.'
'Included makefile 'xxx' was not found.'
> A makefile specified on the command line (first form) or included (second form) was not found.

'warning: overriding commands for target 'xxx''
'warning: ignoring old commands for target 'xxx''
> GNU make allows commands to be specified only once per target (except for double-colon rules). If you give commands for a target which already has been defined to have commands, this warning is issued and the second set of commands will overwrite the first set.

'Circular xxx <- yyy dependency dropped.'
> This means that make detected a loop in the dependency graph: after tracing the dependency yyy of target xxx, and its dependencies, etc., one of them depended on xxx again.

'Recursive variable 'xxx' references itself (eventually). Stop.'
> This means you've defined a normal (recursive) make variable xxx that, when its expanded, will refer to itself (xxx). This is not allowed; either use simply-expanded variables (:=) or use the append operator (+=).

'Unterminated variable reference. Stop.'
> This means you forgot to provide the proper closing parenthesis or brace in your variable or function reference.

'insufficient arguments to function 'xxx'. Stop.'
> This means you haven't provided the requisite number of arguments for this function. See the documentation of the function for a description of its arguments.

'missing target pattern. Stop.'
'multiple target patterns. Stop.'
'target pattern contains no '%'. Stop.'
> These are generated for malformed static pattern rules. The first means there's no pattern in the target section of the rule, the second means there are multiple patterns in the target section, and the third means the target doesn't contain a pattern character (%).

Appendix C Complex Makefile Example

Here is the makefile for the GNU `tar` program. This is a moderately complex makefile.

Because it is the first target, the default goal is 'all'. An interesting feature of this makefile is that 'testpad.h' is a source file automatically created by the `testpad` program, itself compiled from 'testpad.c'.

If you type 'make' or 'make all', then make creates the 'tar' executable, the 'rmt' daemon that provides remote tape access, and the 'tar.info' Info file.

If you type 'make install', then make not only creates 'tar', 'rmt', and 'tar.info', but also installs them.

If you type 'make clean', then make removes the '.o' files, and the 'tar', 'rmt', 'testpad', 'testpad.h', and 'core' files.

If you type 'make distclean', then make not only removes the same files as does 'make clean' but also the 'TAGS', 'Makefile', and 'config.status' files. (Although it is not evident, this makefile (and 'config.status') is generated by the user with the `configure` program, which is provided in the `tar` distribution, but is not shown here.)

If you type 'make realclean', then make removes the same files as does 'make distclean' and also removes the Info files generated from 'tar.texinfo'.

In addition, there are targets `shar` and `dist` that create distribution kits.

```
# Generated automatically from Makefile.in by configure.
# Un*x Makefile for GNU tar program.
# Copyright (C) 1991 Free Software Foundation, Inc.

# This program is free software; you can redistribute
# it and/or modify it under the terms of the GNU
# General Public License ...
...
...
SHELL = /bin/sh

#### Start of system configuration section. ####

srcdir = .
```

```
# If you use gcc, you should either run the
# fixincludes script that comes with it or else use
# gcc with the -traditional option.  Otherwise ioctl
# calls will be compiled incorrectly on some systems.
CC = gcc -O
YACC = bison -y
INSTALL = /usr/local/bin/install -c
INSTALLDATA = /usr/local/bin/install -c -m 644
# Things you might add to DEFS:
# -DSTDC_HEADERS         If you have ANSI C headers and
#                        libraries.
# -DPOSIX                If you have POSIX.1 headers and
#                        libraries.
# -DBSD42                If you have sys/dir.h (unless
#                        you use -DPOSIX), sys/file.h,
#                        and st_blocks in 'struct stat'.
# -DUSG                  If you have System V/ANSI C
#                        string and memory functions
#                        and headers, sys/sysmacros.h,
#                        fcntl.h, getcwd, no valloc,
#                        and ndir.h (unless
#                        you use -DDIRENT).
# -DNO_MEMORY_H          If USG or STDC_HEADERS but do not
#                        include memory.h.
# -DDIRENT               If USG and you have dirent.h
#                        instead of ndir.h.
# -DSIGTYPE=int          If your signal handlers
#                        return int, not void.
# -DNO_MTIO              If you lack sys/mtio.h
#                        (magtape ioctls).
# -DNO_REMOTE            If you do not have a remote shell
#                        or rexec.
# -DUSE_REXEC            To use rexec for remote tape
#                        operations instead of
#                        forking rsh or remsh.
# -DVPRINTF_MISSING      If you lack vprintf function
#                        (but have _doprnt).
# -DDOPRNT_MISSING       If you lack _doprnt function.
#                        Also need to define
#                        -DVPRINTF_MISSING.
# -DFTIME_MISSING        If you lack ftime system call.
# -DSTRSTR_MISSING       If you lack strstr function.
```

```
# -DVALLOC_MISSING        If you lack valloc function.
# -DMKDIR_MISSING         If you lack mkdir and
#                         rmdir system calls.
# -DRENAME_MISSING        If you lack rename system call.
# -DFTRUNCATE_MISSING     If you lack ftruncate
#                         system call.
# -DV7                    On Version 7 Unix (not
#                         tested in a long time).
# -DEMUL_OPEN3            If you lack a 3-argument version
#                         of open, and want to emulate it
#                         with system calls you do have.
# -DNO_OPEN3              If you lack the 3-argument open
#                         and want to disable the tar -k
#                         option instead of emulating open.
# -DXENIX                 If you have sys/inode.h
#                         and need it 94 to be included.

DEFS =  -DSIGTYPE=int -DDIRENT -DSTRSTR_MISSING \
        -DVPRINTF_MISSING -DBSD42
# Set this to rtapelib.o unless you defined NO_REMOTE,
# in which case make it empty.
RTAPELIB = rtapelib.o
LIBS =
DEF_AR_FILE = /dev/rmt8
DEFBLOCKING = 20

CDEBUG = -g
CFLAGS = $(CDEBUG) -I. -I$(srcdir) $(DEFS) \
        -DDEF_AR_FILE=\"$(DEF_AR_FILE)\" \
        -DDEFBLOCKING=$(DEFBLOCKING)
LDFLAGS = -g

prefix = /usr/local
# Prefix for each installed program,
# normally empty or 'g'.
binprefix =

# The directory to install tar in.
bindir = $(prefix)/bin

# The directory to install the info files in.
infodir = $(prefix)/info

#### End of system configuration section. ####
```

```
SRC1 =  tar.c create.c extract.c buffer.c \
        getoldopt.c update.c gnu.c mangle.c
SRC2 =  version.c list.c names.c diffarch.c \
        port.c wildmat.c getopt.c
SRC3 =  getopt1.c regex.c getdate.y
SRCS =  $(SRC1) $(SRC2) $(SRC3)
OBJ1 =  tar.o create.o extract.o buffer.o \
        getoldopt.o update.o gnu.o mangle.o
OBJ2 =  version.o list.o names.o diffarch.o \
        port.o wildmat.o getopt.o
OBJ3 =  getopt1.o regex.o getdate.o $(RTAPELIB)
OBJS =  $(OBJ1) $(OBJ2) $(OBJ3)
AUX =   README COPYING ChangeLog Makefile.in \
        makefile.pc configure configure.in \
        tar.texinfo tar.info* texinfo.tex \
        tar.h port.h open3.h getopt.h regex.h \
        rmt.h rmt.c rtapelib.c alloca.c \
        msd_dir.h msd_dir.c tcexparg.c \
        level-0 level-1 backup-specs testpad.c

all:    tar rmt tar.info

tar:    $(OBJS)
        $(CC) $(LDFLAGS) -o $@ $(OBJS) $(LIBS)

rmt:    rmt.c
        $(CC) $(CFLAGS) $(LDFLAGS) -o $@ rmt.c

tar.info: tar.texinfo
        makeinfo tar.texinfo

install: all
        $(INSTALL) tar $(bindir)/$(binprefix)tar
        -test ! -f rmt || $(INSTALL) rmt /etc/rmt
        $(INSTALLDATA) $(srcdir)/tar.info* $(infodir)

$(OBJS): tar.h port.h testpad.h
regex.o buffer.o tar.o: regex.h
# getdate.y has 8 shift/reduce conflicts.

testpad.h: testpad
        ./testpad

testpad: testpad.o
        $(CC) -o $@ testpad.o
```

```
TAGS:    $(SRCS)
         etags $(SRCS)

clean:
         rm -f *.o tar rmt testpad testpad.h core

distclean: clean
         rm -f TAGS Makefile config.status

realclean: distclean
         rm -f tar.info*

shar: $(SRCS) $(AUX)
         shar $(SRCS) $(AUX) | compress \
           > tar-'sed -e '/version_string/!d' \
                   -e 's/[^0-9.]*\([0-9.]*\).*/\1/' \
                   -e q
                   version.c'.shar.Z

dist: $(SRCS) $(AUX)
         echo tar-'sed \
             -e '/version_string/!d' \
             -e 's/[^0-9.]*\([0-9.]*\).*/\1/' \
             -e q
             version.c' > .fname
         -rm -rf 'cat .fname'
         mkdir 'cat .fname'
         ln $(SRCS) $(AUX) 'cat .fname'
         -rm -rf 'cat .fname' .fname
         tar chZf 'cat .fname'.tar.Z 'cat .fname'

tar.zoo: $(SRCS) $(AUX)
         -rm -rf tmp.dir
         -mkdir tmp.dir
         -rm tar.zoo
         for X in $(SRCS) $(AUX) ; do \
             echo $$X ; \
             sed 's/$$/^M/' $$X \
             > tmp.dir/$$X ; done
         cd tmp.dir ; zoo aM ../tar.zoo *
         -rm -rf tmp.dir
```

Index of Concepts

#

\# (comments), in commands 37
\# (comments), in makefile 11
`#include` 34

$

\$, in function call 71
\$, in rules 17
\$, in variable name 55
\$, in variable reference 51

%

%, in pattern rules 104
%, quoting in `patsubst` 72
%, quoting in static pattern 32
%, quoting in `vpath` 22
%, quoting with \ (backslash) . . . 22, 32, 72

*

* (wildcard character) 18

'

,v (RCS file extension) 99

-

- (in commands) 41
-, and `define` 48
`--assume-new` 86, 92
`--assume-new`, and recursion 46
`--assume-old` 87, 91
`--assume-old`, and recursion 46
`--debug` 89
`--directory` 43, 89
`--directory`, and `--print-directory`
. . . . 48
`--directory`, and recursion 46
`--dry-run` 37, 85, 90
`--environment-overrides` 89
`--file` 12, 83, 89
`--file`, and recursion 46

`--help` 90
`--ignore-errors` 41, 90
`--include-dir` 13, 90
`--jobs` 39, 90
`--jobs`, and recursion 46
`--just-print` 37, 85, 90
`--keep-going` 41, 88, 90
`--load-average` 40, 90
`--makefile` 12, 83, 89
`--max-load` 40, 90
`--new-file` 86, 92
`--new-file`, and recursion 46
`--no-builtin-rules` 91
`--no-keep-going` 91
`--no-print-directory` 48, 92
`--old-file` 87, 91
`--old-file`, and recursion 46
`--print-data-base` 91
`--print-directory` 92
`--print-directory`, and `--directory`
. . . . 48
`--print-directory`, and recursion 48
`--print-directory`, disabling 48
`--question` 86, 91
`--quiet` 37, 91
`--recon` 37, 85, 90
`--silent` 37, 91
`--stop` 91
`--touch` 85, 92
`--touch`, and recursion 43
`--version` 92
`--warn-undefined-variables` 93
`--what-if` 86, 92
-b 89
-C 43, 89
-C, and -w 48
-C, and recursion 46
-d 89
-e 89
-e (shell flag) 35
-f 12, 83, 89

-f, and recursion...................... 46
-h.. 90
-i... 41, 90
-I... 13, 90
-j... 39, 90
-j, and archive update.............. 117
-j, and recursion..................... 46
-k....................................... 41, 88, 90
-l.. 90
-l (library search) 25
-l (load average)...................... 40
-m.. 89
-M (to compiler)...................... 34
-MM (to GNU compiler)............... 35
-n 37, 85, 90
-o 87, 91
-o, and recursion..................... 46
-p 91
-q... 86, 91
-r 91
-s.. 37, 91
-S 91
-t 85, 92
-t, and recursion..................... 43
-v 92
-w 92
-W... 86, 92
-w, and -C 48
-w, and recursion..................... 48
-W, and recursion..................... 46
-w, disabling......................... 48

.

.a (archives) 117
.c 97
.C 97
.cc 97
.ch 99
.d 35
.def 97
.dvi 99
.f 97
.F 97
.info...................................... 99

.l 98
.ln 99
.mod 97
.o 97, 98
.p 97
.PRECIOUS intermediate files.......... 103
.r 97
.s 98
.S 98
.sh 100
.sym 97
.tex 99
.texi 99
.texinfo 99
.txinfo 99
.w 99
.web 99
.y 98

:

:: rules (double-colon) 34
:=.............................. 53, 58

=

=.............................. 52, 58

?

? (wildcard character)................ 18
?=.............................. 54, 58

@

@ (in commands) 37
@, and define 48

[

[...] (wildcard characters) 18

_

__.SYMDEF 116

~

~ (tilde)............................... 18

+

+, and define 48
+= 59

\

\ (backslash), for continuation lines 4
\ (backslash), in commands 38
\ (backslash), to quote % 22, 32, 72

A

algorithm for directory search 23
all (standard target) 84
appending to variables 59
ar 101
archive 115
archive member targets 115
archive symbol directory updating 116
archive, and -j 117
archive, and parallel execution 117
archive, suffix rule for 117
Arg list too long 46
arguments of functions 71
as 98, 101
assembly, rule to compile 98
automatic generation of dependencies
.... 13, 34
automatic variables 106

B

backquotes 81
backslash (\), for continuation lines 4
backslash (\), in commands 38
backslash (\), to quote % 22, 32, 72
backslashes in pathnames and wildcard
expansion 20
basename 76
binary packages 138
broken pipe 40
bugs, reporting 2
built-in special targets 28

C

C, rule to compile 97

C++, rule to compile 97
cc 97, 101
cd (shell command) 38, 43
chains of rules 102
check (standard target) 85
clean (standard target) 84
clean target 5, 9
cleaning up 9
clobber (standard target) 85
co 99, 101
combining rules by dependency 8
command line variable definitions, and
recursion 46
command line variables 87
commands 17
commands, backslash (\) in 38
commands, comments in 37
commands, echoing 37
commands, empty 49
commands, errors in 40
commands, execution 38
commands, execution in parallel 39
commands, expansion 81
commands, how to write 37
commands, instead of executing 85
commands, introduction to 3
commands, quoting newlines in 38
commands, sequences of 48
comments, in commands 37
comments, in makefile 11
compatibility 119
compatibility in exporting 45
compilation, testing 88
computed variable name 55
conditional variable assignment 54
conditionals 65
continuation lines 4
conventions for makefiles 125
ctangle 99, 101
cweave 99, 101

D

deducing commands (implicit rules) 7

default directries for included makefiles
.... 13
default goal........................ 5, 17
default makefile name................ 11
default rules, last-resort.............. 110
defining variables verbatim............ 61
deletion of target files.............. 41, 42
dependencies.......................... 18
dependencies, automatic generation . . . 13,
    34
dependencies, introduction to.......... 3
dependencies, list of all.............. 106
dependencies, list of changed 106
dependencies, varying (static pattern)
.... 31
dependency 17
dependency pattern, implicit 104
dependency pattern, static (not implicit)
.... 32
directive 11
directories, printing them............. 47
directories, updating archive symbol.. 116
directory part....................... 75
directory search (VPATH).............. 21
directory search (VPATH), and implicit
    rules 24
directory search (VPATH), and link libraries
.... 25
directory search (VPATH), and shell
    commands....................... 24
directory search algorithm............. 23
directory search, traditional 23
dist (standard target) 85
distclean (standard target).......... 85
dollar sign ($), in function call......... 71
dollar sign ($), in rules 17
dollar sign ($), in variable name 55
dollar sign ($), in variable reference.... 51
double-colon rules.................... 34
duplicate words, removing............. 74

E

E2BIG.............................. 46
echoing of commands................. 37

editor.................................. 3
Emacs (M-x compile) 41
empty commands 49
empty targets 27
environment 62
environment, and recursion........... 44
environment, SHELL in................ 39
errors (in commands) 40
errors with wildcards................. 19
execution, in parallel 39
execution, instead of 85
execution, of commands.............. 38
exit status (errors) 40
explicit rule, definition of............. 11
exporting variables................... 44

F

f77 .... 97, 101
features of GNU make............... 119
features, missing 123
file name functions 75
file name of makefile 11
file name of makefile, how to specify ... 12
file name prefix, adding 76
file name suffix...................... 76
file name suffix, adding............... 76
file name with wildcards.............. 18
file name, basename of 76
file name, directory part............. 75
file name, nondirectory part 75
files, assuming new 86
files, assuming old................... 87
files, avoiding recompilation of........ 87
files, intermediate 102
filtering out words................... 74
filtering words....................... 74
finding strings....................... 74
flags 89
flags for compilers................... 100
flavors of variables 52
FORCE.............................. 27
force targets 27
Fortran, rule to compile 97
functions............................ 71

functions, for file names 75
functions, for text 72
functions, syntax of 71

G

g++ 97, 101
gcc 97
generating dependencies automatically
.... 13, 34
get 99, 101
globbing (wildcards) 18
goal 5
goal, default 5, 17
goal, how to specify 83

H

home directory 18

I

IEEE Standard 1003.2 1
implicit rule 95
implicit rule, and directory search 24
implicit rule, and VPATH 24
implicit rule, definition of 11
implicit rule, how to use 95
implicit rule, introduction to 7
implicit rule, predefined 96
implicit rule, search algorithm 112
included makefiles, default directries ... 13
including (MAKEFILES variable) 13
including other makefiles 12
incompatibilities 123
Info, rule to format 99
install (standard target) 85
intermediate files 102
intermediate files, preserving 103
intermediate targets, explicit 28
interrupt 42

J

job slots 39
job slots, and recursion 46
jobs, limiting based on load 40
joining lists of words 77

K

killing (interruption) 42

L

last-resort default rules 110
ld 98
lex 98, 101
Lex, rule to run 98
libraries for linking, directory search ... 25
library archive, suffix rule for 117
limiting jobs based on load 40
link libraries, and directory search 25
linking, predefined rule for 98
lint 99
lint, rule to run 99
list of all dependencies 106
list of changed dependencies 106
load average 40
loops in variable expansion 53
lpr (shell command) 19, 27

M

m2c 97
macro 51
make depend 35
MAKECMDGOALS 84
makefile 3
makefile name 11
makefile name, how to specify 12
makefile rule parts 3
makefile, and MAKEFILES variable 13
makefile, conventions for 125
makefile, how make processes 5
makefile, how to write 11
makefile, including 12
makefile, overriding 15
makefile, remaking of 14
makefile, simple 4
makeinfo 99, 101
match-anything rule 109
match-anything rule, used to override .. 15
missing features 123
mistakes with wildcards 19

modified variable reference 55
Modula-2, rule to compile 97
mostlyclean (standard target) 85
multiple rules for one target 30
multiple rules for one target (::) 34
multiple targets 30
multiple targets, in pattern rule 105

N

name of makefile 11
name of makefile, how to specify 12
nested variable reference 55
newline, quoting, in commands 38
newline, quoting, in makefile 4
nondirectory part 75

O

obj 6
OBJ 6
objects 6
OBJECTS 6
objs 6
OBJS 6
old-fashioned suffix rules 111
options 89
options, and recursion 46
options, setting from environment 47
options, setting in makefiles 47
order of pattern rules 105
origin of variable 79
overriding makefiles 15
overriding variables with arguments . . . 87
overriding with override 61

P

parallel execution 39
parallel execution, and archive update
. . . . 117
parts of makefile rule 3
Pascal, rule to compile 97
pattern rule 104
pattern rules, order of 105
pattern rules, static (not implicit) 31
pattern rules, static, syntax of 31

pattern-specific variables 64
pc 97, 101
phony targets 25
pitfalls of wildcards 19
portability 119
POSIX 1
POSIX.2 46
post-installation commands 137
pre-installation commands 137
precious targets 28
prefix, adding 76
preserving intermediate files 103
preserving with .PRECIOUS 28, 103
preserving with .SECONDARY 29
print (standard target) 85
print target 19, 27
printing directories 47
printing of commands 37
problems and bugs, reporting 2
problems with wildcards 19
processing a makefile 5

Q

question mode 86
quoting %, in patsubst 72
quoting %, in static pattern 32
quoting %, in vpath 22
quoting newline, in commands 38
quoting newline, in makefile 4

R

Ratfor, rule to compile 97
RCS, rule to extract from 99
README 11
realclean (standard target) 85
recompilation 3
recompilation, avoiding 87
recording events with empty targets . . . 27
recursion 42
recursion, and -C 46
recursion, and -f 46
recursion, and -j 46
recursion, and -o 46
recursion, and -t 43

recursion, and -w...................... 48
recursion, and -W...................... 46
recursion, and command line variable
    definitions........................ 46
recursion, and environment........... 44
recursion, and MAKE variable.......... 43
recursion, and MAKEFILES variable..... 14
recursion, and options................ 46
recursion, and printing directories..... 47
recursion, and variables............... 44
recursion, level of.................... 45
recursive variable expansion....... 51, 52
recursively expanded variables........ 52
reference to variables.............. 51, 55
relinking............................. 6
remaking makefiles................... 14
removal of target files.............. 41, 42
removing duplicate words............. 74
removing, to clean up................. 9
reporting bugs........................ 2
rm.................................. 101
rm (shell command)........ 5, 19, 25, 41
rule commands........................ 37
rule dependencies.................... 18
rule syntax.......................... 17
rule targets......................... 17
rule, and $.......................... 17
rule, double-colon (::)............... 34
rule, explicit, definition of............ 11
rule, how to write.................... 17
rule, implicit........................ 95
rule, implicit, and directory search..... 24
rule, implicit, and VPATH.............. 24
rule, implicit, chains of.............. 102
rule, implicit, definition of............ 11
rule, implicit, how to use.............. 95
rule, implicit, introduction to.......... 7
rule, implicit, predefined.............. 96
rule, introduction to.................. 3
rule, multiple for one target.......... 30
rule, no commands or dependencies.... 27
rule, pattern........................ 104
rule, static pattern.................. 31
rule, static pattern versus implicit..... 33

rule, with multiple targets............. 30

S

s. (SCCS file prefix).................. 99
SCCS, rule to extract from........... 99
search algorithm, implicit rule........ 112
search path for dependencies (VPATH).. 21
search path for dependencies (VPATH), and
    implicit rules.................... 24
search path for dependencies (VPATH), and
    link libraries..................... 25
searching for strings.................. 74
secondary files...................... 103
secondary targets.................... 29
sed (shell command).................. 35
selecting a word..................... 77
selecting word lists.................. 77
sequences of commands............... 48
setting options from environment...... 47
setting options in makefiles........... 47
setting variables..................... 58
several rules for one target........... 30
several targets in a rule.............. 30
shar (standard target)............... 85
shell command....................... 5
shell command, and directory search... 24
shell command, execution............. 38
shell command, function for........... 81
shell file name pattern (in include)... 12
shell wildcards (in include).......... 12
SHELL, MS-DOS specifics.............. 38
signal.............................. 42
silent operation..................... 37
simple makefile...................... 4
simple variable expansion............. 51
simplifying with variables............. 6
simply expanded variables............. 53
sorting words........................ 74
spaces, in variable values............. 54
spaces, stripping.................... 73
special targets...................... 28
specifying makefile name............. 12
standard input...................... 40
standards conformance................ 1

standards for makefiles 125
static pattern rule 31
static pattern rule, syntax of 31
static pattern rule, versus implicit 33
stem 31, 108
stem, variable for 107
strings, searching for 74
stripping whitespace 73
sub-**make** 44
subdirectories, recursion for 42
substitution variable reference 55
suffix rule 111
suffix rule, for archive 117
suffix, adding 76
suffix, function to find 76
suffix, substituting in variables 55
switches 89
symbol directories, updating archive . . 116
syntax of rules 17

T

tab character (in commands) 17
tabs in rules 3
TAGS (standard target) 85
tangle 99, 101
tar (standard target) 85
target 17
target pattern, implicit 104
target pattern, static (not implicit) 31
target, deleting on error 41
target, deleting on interrupt 42
target, multiple in pattern rule 105
target, multiple rules for one 30
target, touching 85
target-specific variables 63
targets 17
targets without a file 25
targets, built-in special 28
targets, empty 27
targets, force 27
targets, introduction to 3
targets, multiple 30
targets, phony 25
terminal rule 109

test (standard target) 85
testing compilation 88
tex 99, 101
TEX, rule to run 99
texi2dvi 99, 101
Texinfo, rule to format 99
tilde (~) 18
touch (shell command) 19, 27
touching files 85
traditional directory search 23

U

undefined variables, warning message . . 93
updating archive symbol directories . . 116
updating makefiles 14

V

value 51
value, how a variable gets it 58
variable 51
variable definition 11
variables 6
variables, '$' in name 55
variables, and implicit rule 106
variables, appending to 59
variables, automatic 106
variables, command line 87
variables, command line, and recursion
. . . . 46
variables, computed names 55
variables, conditional assignment 54
variables, defining verbatim 61
variables, environment 44, 62
variables, exporting 44
variables, flavors 52
variables, how they get their values 58
variables, how to reference 51
variables, loops in expansion 53
variables, modified reference 55
variables, nested references 55
variables, origin of 79
variables, overriding 61
variables, overriding with arguments . . . 87
variables, pattern-specific 64

variables, recursively expanded 52
variables, setting 58
variables, simply expanded 53
variables, spaces in values 54
variables, substituting suffix in 55
variables, substitution reference 55
variables, target-specific 63
variables, warning for undefined 93
varying dependencies 31
verbatim variable definition 61
vpath 21
VPATH, and implicit rules 24
VPATH, and link libraries 25

W

weave 99, 101
Web, rule to run 99
what if 86
whitespace, in variable values 54
whitespace, stripping 73
wildcard 18

wildcard pitfalls 19
wildcard, function 78
wildcard, in archive member 115
wildcard, in **include** 12
wildcards and MS-DOS/MS-Windows
     backslashes 20
word, selecting a 77
words, extracting first 77
words, filtering 74
words, filtering out 74
words, finding number 77
words, iterating over 78
words, joining lists 77
words, removing duplicates 74
words, selecting lists of 77
writing rule commands 37
writing rules 17

Y

yacc 48, 98, 101
Yacc, rule to run 98

Index of Functions, Variables, & Directives

$

$% 106
$(%D) 107
$(%F) 107
$(*D) 107
$(*F) 107
$(?D) 108
$(?F) 108
$(@D) 107
$(@F) 107
$(^D) 108
$(^F) 108
$(<D) 108
$(<F) 108
$* 106
$*, and static pattern 33
$? 106
$@ 106
$+ 106
$^ 106
$< 106

%

% (automatic variable) 106
%D (automatic variable) 107
%F (automatic variable) 107

*

* (automatic variable) 106
* (automatic variable), unsupported
        bizarre usage 123
*D (automatic variable) 107
*F (automatic variable) 107

.

.DEFAULT 28, 110
.DEFAULT, and empty commands 49
.DELETE_ON_ERROR 41
.EXPORT_ALL_VARIABLES 29, 45

.IGNORE 29, 41
.INTERMEDIATE 28
.PHONY 25, 28
.POSIX 46
.PRECIOUS 28, 42
.SECONDARY 29
.SILENT 29, 37
.SUFFIXES 28, 112

/

/usr/gnu/include 13
/usr/include 13
/usr/local/include 13

?

? (automatic variable) 106
?D (automatic variable) 108
?F (automatic variable) 108

@

@ (automatic variable) 106
@D (automatic variable) 107
@F (automatic variable) 107

+

+ (automatic variable) 106

^

^ (automatic variable) 106
^D (automatic variable) 108
^F (automatic variable) 108

<

< (automatic variable) 106
<D (automatic variable) 108
<F (automatic variable) 108

A

addprefix 76
addsuffix 76
AR 101
ARFLAGS 102
AS 101
ASFLAGS 102

B

basename 76

C

CC 101
CFLAGS 102
CO 101
COFLAGS 102
COMSPEC 38
CPP 101
CPPFLAGS 102
CTANGLE 101
CWEAVE 101
CXX 101
CXXFLAGS 102

D

define 61
dir 75

E

else 66
endef 61
endif 66
export 44

F

FC 101
FFLAGS 102
filter 74
filter-out 74
findstring 74
firstword 77
foreach 78

G

GET 101
GFLAGS 102
GNUmakefile 11
GPATH 23

I

ifdef 66
ifeq 66
ifndef 66
ifneq 66
include 12

J

join 77

L

LDFLAGS 102
LEX 101
LFLAGS 102

M

MAKE 43, 53
MAKECMDGOALS 84
makefile 11
Makefile 11
MAKEFILES 13, 45
MAKEFLAGS 46
MAKEINFO 101
MAKELEVEL 45, 53
MAKEOVERRIDES 46
MFLAGS 47

N

notdir 75

O

origin 79
OUTPUT_OPTION 100
override 61

P

patsubst 55, 72
PC 101
PFLAGS 102

R

RFLAGS 102
RM 101

S

shell 81
SHELL 38
SHELL (command execution) 38
sort 74
strip 73
subst 30, 72
suffix 76
SUFFIXES 112

T

TANGLE 101

U

unexport 44

V

vpath 21
VPATH 21

W

WEAVE 101
wildcard 20, 78
word 77
wordlist 77
words 77

TEX

TEX 101
TEXI2DVI 101

Y

YACC 101
YACCR 101
YFLAGS 102

Available from the Free Software Foundation...

This is a list of items available from the Free Software Foundation as of the publication of this manual. New items may not yet appear on this list. Please consult our web site at http://www.gnu.org for current information and pricing, or contact our office and ask for a GNU's Bulletin.

BOOKS:

- **GNU Software for MS-Windows and MS-DOS** 108 pp. + CD-ROM.
- **GNU Emacs Manual** For text editing and programming. 528 pp.
- **Using and Porting GNU CC** C, C++, & Objective C compiler. 545 pp.
- **Debugging with GDB** How to use the GNU Debugger. 192 pp.
- **GNU Make** Extensions, writing makefiles, reference. 158 pp.
- **The Bison Manual** YACC-compatible parser generator. 104 pp.
- **GNU Emacs Lisp Reference Manual** A complete guide. 888 pp.
- **Programming in Emacs Lisp: An Introduction** Customization. 257 pp.
- **GAWK: The GNU Awk User's Guide** Easy text processing. 324 pp.
- **Texinfo** Producing printed and online GNU documentation. 256 pp.
- **GNU C Library Reference Manual** A comprehensive guide. 674 pp.
- **Flex: The Lexical Scanner Generator** The GNU version of lex. 120 pp.
- **Termcap Manual** Display terminal data base library. 64 pp.
- **Calc Manual** An Emacs package for advanced mathematics. 572 pp.

OTHER ITEMS:

- **GNU Source Code CD-ROM** - All the GNU project code - 2 disks.
- **GNU Compiler Tools Binaries CD-ROM** - Contains executables for many systems for the GNU C compiler (GCC), the GNU Fortran compiler (G77), and the GNU compiler tool set (Binutils, Bison, Flex, GDB, Make). See http://www.gnu.org for details.
- **Reference cards** - available for Emacs, Calc, GDB, Flex, and Bison.
- **GNU T-shirts**

All purchases made from the FSF help support the development of more free software and documentation. The Free Software Foundation is a 501 (c) 3 not-for-profit corporation, and donations are tax-deductible in the U.S.

Free Software Foundation, 59 Temple Place, Suite 330, Boston, MA 02111
+1-617-542-5942 Fax: +1-617-542-2652 gnu@gnu.org http://www.gnu.org